CASEWORK
IN THE
CHILD CARE SERVICE

ENGLAND: BUTTERWORTH & CO. (PUBLISHERS) LTD.
                LONDON: 88 Kingsway, W.C.2.
AFRICA: BUTTERWORTH & CO. (AFRICA) LTD.
                DURBAN: 33/35 Beach Grove
AUSTRALIA: BUTTERWORTH & CO. (AUSTRALIA) LTD.
                SYDNEY: 6/8 O'Connell Street
                MELBOURNE: 473 Bourke Street
                BRISBANE: 240 Queen Street
CANADA: BUTTERWORTH & CO. (CANADA) LTD.
                TORONTO: 1367 Danforth Avenue, 6
NEW ZEALAND: BUTTERWORTH & CO. (NEW ZEALAND) LTD.
                WELLINGTON: 49/51 Ballance Street
                AUCKLAND: 35 High Street
U.S.A.:   BUTTERWORTH INC.
                WASHINGTON, D.C.: 7235 Wisconsin Avenue, 14

CASEWORK

IN THE

CHILD CARE SERVICE

BY

NOEL TIMMS, M.A.

*Associate of the Association of
Psychiatric Social Workers*

*Lecturer in Social Work in the Faculty
of Commerce and Social Science,
University of Birmingham*

LONDON

BUTTERWORTHS

1962

©
BUTTERWORTH & CO. (PUBLISHERS) LTD.
1962

*Printed in Great Britain by
Spottiswoode, Ballantyne and Co. Ltd.
London and Colchester*

R7246

PREFACE

The Child Care Service is a young institution. It was established in 1948, though social work on behalf of children has a much longer history. Now that the exploratory phase of the new service is over and its identity has been at least partly established, child care workers are anxious to increase its efficiency, and to develop their own professional skill. Many workers who are untrained or only partially trained wish to further their knowledge and understanding of child care and to improve their practice. Trained workers complain of the lack of stimulation and discussion, due to a shortage of literature relevant to the work of the child care officer. J. S. Heywood's *Children in Care* (Routledge and Kegan Paul, 1959) is a useful introductory description of the historical background of the Service, and popular studies have been published of adoption (e.g., M. Kornitzer, *Adoption*, Putman, 1959), psychology for child care workers (e.g., A. H. Bowley, *Child Care: A Handbook on the Care of the Child deprived of a normal Home Life*, Livingstone, 1951), and of foster care (e.g., J. Balls, *Where Love Is*, Gollancz, 1958). Yet there is little writing in this country that actually helps child care officers in their work, apart from Britton's essential article "Casework Techniques in Child-Care Services", published in the January, 1955, issue of *Case Conference*, and Trasler's recent book, *In Place of Parents*, published by Routledge and Kegan Paul in 1960. In fact, as Chapter 8 illustrates, there are elements of contradiction and unreality in some of the writings so far published.

This book is an attempt to provide a simple account of the essentials of casework in the child care setting. It is not an analysis of the general work of Children's Departments. What is envisaged is some practical help in understanding and interviewing illustrated by case material, an introduction to some general notions on child care collected in a convenient and relevant form. It is hoped that this introductory text might also prove of use to students placed in child care agencies as part of their fieldwork. Finally, if the book succeeds in stimulating the more seasoned professional by the presentation of some problems in a version different from her own, it will have served its purpose.

The book has the following plan. A short historical introduction shows something of the traditions of social casework, and the way in which its important components have developed. Chapter 2 is concerned with the problem of admission to care, in a voluntary or compulsory form. Chapters 3 and 4 deal with casework service to the child and to the adolescent. Chapters 5 and 6 are concerned with the help that can be given to foster parents. Chapter 7 deals with casework with families, and a final chapter discusses the child care officer herself. An attempt has been made to cover the most important aspects of the work of the service, but problems of adoption have been excluded from this book. These have been discussed at length in other works and problems of confidentiality make this an especially difficult area from which to obtain case material.

The book relies considerably upon the presentation of case material from Children's Departments. Cases have been chosen to illustrate common casework problems and a range of possible responses on the part of child care officers; they are not presented as a cross-section of the work of Children's Departments nor as yielding any indication of its general quality. The case material has, of course, been disguised and it has been decided, in consultation with the departments concerned, that no particular acknowledgments should be made so that confidentiality might be more fully secured. This means that the staff and committees who have contributed case illustrations cannot receive public thanks for their help, save in the most general way. That this acknowledgment must be anonymous does not detract from my warm recognition of the value of their contribution to this book.

Personal acknowledgment should be given to the following who have greatly assisted by reading the manuscript and offering critical comment and advice: Mrs. M. Decker (Children's Officer, Preston), Mrs. E. E. Irvine (Senior Tutor, Tavistock Clinic), my colleague Mrs. P. Shapiro, Mr. K. Brill (Children's Officer, Devon), Professor F. Itzin (Iowa University, U.S.A.). None of the above, of course, is responsible for what follows. Some of the case examples and some of the discussion in Chapters 3, 5 and 6 are based on material already published in *Case Conference*. I would like to thank the Editor, Mrs. K. McDougall, for permission to use this material.

Birmingham,   NOEL TIMMS
May, 1962.

TABLE OF CONTENTS

PAGE

PREFACE v

CHAPTER

1 WHAT IS CASEWORK? 1

The Social Agency 4
Work on Cases Governed by Certain Principles . . 6
Knowledge 11
Skill in Human Relationships 16

2 ADMISSION TO CARE 21

Application I 24
Application II 27
Application III 31

3 CASEWORK WITH CHILDREN 38

Childhood Development 42
Skill and Objectives in Casework with Children . . 48

(i) *Jean and Sandra* 51
(ii) *Beryl and Jennifer* 52
(iii) *Gwen* 53
(iv) *Matthew* 54
(v) *Robert* 55
(vi) *Muriel* 56

4 CASEWORK WITH THE ADOLESCENT . . . 59

General Description 60
Betty 63
General Principles of Casework Help for Adolescents . . 68

The Families of Adolescents are Important 68
The Crises of Conscience 71
The Problem of Identity 74
Problems in Taking Help 76

5 FOSTER PARENTS AND THE CHILD CARE OFFICER
   (1) 79

Choosing Foster Parents 83
General Knowledge 84
Knowledge of the Individual Applicant 88
Skill in Selection 93
Three Situations 96
Rejection 100

vii

CHAPTER   PAGE

6 FOSTER PARENTS AND THE CHILD CARE OFFICER
   (2)   101
   Problems   101
      (a) *Adequacy*   102
      (b) *Rivalry*.   103
      (c) *Control*   104
   Ways of Helping   106
      (i) *The Worker's Own Attitude*   106
      (ii) *The Relationship between Worker and Foster Parents*   .   109
   The Beginning of Foster Care   115
   Help from Other Sources   119
   Placement in the Maladjusted School   122

7 WORKING WITH FAMILIES   124
      (i) Helping Families to Part with their Children   .   .   124
      (ii) Helping Families to Regain Care of their Children   .   131
      (iii) Helping Families to Retain Care of their Children   .   134
   The Family as a Whole   139
   Co-operation   140
   Help has to be offered with Persistence and with Specific
      Problems   142

8 THE CHILD CARE OFFICER   145
      (i) The Complex Roles of the Child Care Officer   .   .   145
      (ii) Staff Relationships   153
      (iii) Emotional Implications   157

ADDITIONAL READING   161

INDEX   165

CHAPTER 1

WHAT IS CASEWORK?

"Each application for aid or each case of distress should be considered individually not merely in relation to the possibility or desirability of granting an allowance or making a gift—and so closing the matter, but in relation to some purpose or plan which, if it is properly carried out, should produce lasting results. To effect this, the material facts that bear upon the question have to be ascertained ... The causes that have led to distress or want or degradation have to be learnt—not roughly generalized causes merely, such as widowhood, the largeness of a family, illness and the like, but causes, often more potent and less obvious which lie in the character, habits and health of the family itself. From these data some plan of help should be formed."

PooR Law Commission, 1909[1]

"If we scatter relief, how can we pause to see how it tells? How can it spring from that subtle sympathy which feels that to this man or woman gifts will be helpful, to another deadly."

OCTAVIA HILL[2]

CASEWORK is not a new creation, but it is still regarded by some with suspicion and by others hardly at all. Some critics claim that "casework" has corrupted the unsophisticated, but possibly more effective, social worker of the past. Others feel that the term is a simple misnomer for social work and should be abandoned. Many patient and enquiring people are confused by muddle and inadequate scholarship presented as a casework theory. They would sympathize with Octavia Hill's conviction that "there was already too much 'windy talk'; what you wanted was action; for men and women to go and work day by day among the less fortunate".[3] Finally, social workers in departments with apparently well-defined

[1] Appendix, Vol. III. Minutes of Evidence, para. 3 of H. V. Toynbee's evidence.
[2] "The Need of Thoroughness in Charitable Work," *C.O.S. Occasional Papers* 9, Second Series, 1918.
[3] Quoted in Beatrice Webb's *My Apprenticeship*, 1926, p. 278.

functions (such as the Children's Department) may question the relevance of what seems a rarified activity to the pressing realities of their daily routine.

But, what is casework? An introduction to casework in the Child Care Service must obviously describe and demonstrate the relevance of this activity.

The search for an enlightening definition of social casework has never proved very fruitful. In England, for example, it has been seen as the means "by which the occasional needs and misfortunes of individual members of a family are taken as opportunities for strengthening the economic and hygienic position of the whole of it to the utmost extent" (1915);[1] "Our case-work is the outward expression of these underlying beliefs, which may be summed up in the belief in the individual as an individual" (1929);[2] "Casework may be defined as a professional service offered to those who have certain problems of living which they cannot handle unaided. It is the process by which these problems are solved or mitigated" (1955).[3] This is a random selection from a long list of attempted definitions, but it is sufficient to illustrate the pitfalls of an approach to casework by way of definition. These definitions emphasize only particular aspects, the objectives, the general values or the process of help and their inevitable compression reduces their general usefulness even more. It is suggested that the value of definition has probably been overstressed in social work writing and discussion. Most definitions assume that casework is a static principle, an established skill, or a body of organized knowledge that the conscientious may discover if they will. Those who seek to define casework assume that a few happy phrases will indicate firmly the essential nature of casework and, with such a formula established, proceed to discuss casework in the sectional and segmentary fashion that the above quotations reveal.

A more helpful procedure, it is thought, is to bypass the quest for a definition altogether. "Casework" is not a static idea or group of theories that can be defined for all times. The term "casework" represents a group of ideas that have grown, developed and are constantly being modified and changed in some respects. This does

[1] *Annual Report*, Charity Organization Society, 1915/16.
[2] Milnes, N., "Training," *Charity Organization Quarterly*, January, 1929.
[3] Davison, E., "Therapy in Casework," *Social Work*, July, 1955.

not mean that "casework" is too elusive a concept to be identified at all. It is still possible to describe the content of casework in a cogent manner without resorting to an over-ambitious definition. What is required is a practical description that aims at being a working basis for discussion and explanation. Such a starting point is the preamble to the question "What is casework?"

Briefly it is suggested that casework is work on cases guided by certain principles, and the use of knowledge and human relation skills with the object of fulfilling the function of a particular agency. A full exploration of all these elements would require an independent text and all that is possible here is a cursory and selective examination with the particular objectives of this book in mind.

Modern social casework owes its present elements to a long history of growth, experiment and adaptation and this process is still being continued. Any student of casework should be aware of the manner in which casework has developed from its first beginnings. A historical view is important for several reasons. Many of the problems individual workers meet in the course of their present-day work have been experienced already in the course of the profession's growth. It is simply economic to consider this experience and some of the solutions suggested. It is important to understand that casework has some traditions and that these are common to all the social workers in the different special settings. Finally, a historical perspective emphasizes that casework has in the main developed from the continual confrontation of social workers with people in need of help. It is true that on occasions theoretical speculation has become extravagant or sterile, but the starting point for such speculation has been a problem encountered in the field of social work. Helen Bosanquet once stated her conviction on the question of the relationship between theory and practice in the following terms:—

> "Thus, it is my belief that any general notions borrowed from philosophical sources [we could today add, psychological and sociological] which we may use to make our attitude clear to ourselves and the world should be, as they have hitherto been, regarded as secondary and partial—always partial—compared with what is a larger, deeper, and more complex thing, the practical faith embodied in our tradition and in the spirit of our habits of work."[1]

It is to the elucidation of such a tradition that this chapter is directed.

[1] Bosanquet, H., Editorial, *Charity Organization Review*, March, 1921.

The Social Agency

This aspect of casework is considered first because it is extremely difficult to conceive of a caseworker operating outside the framework of the methods and objectives of a social agency, whether this is a voluntary casework society or, for example, a children's department of the local authority. Thus, the beginnings of casework in England are usually seen in the second half of the nineteenth century when social workers were attempting to formulate a clear conception of their methods and objectives. The contribution of the Charity Organization Society is of considerable significance in this respect. The C.O.S., pursuing the general objective of the moral improvement of society, argued that unless some discipline was maintained in the field of relief, overlapping and possibly chaos would ensue. They wanted to make each relief agency conscious of its objectives, and having formulated them to abide by them. They realized that this must involve refusing help to some applicants, as the various relief organizations ceased competing with each other in offering indiscriminate aid. Ultimately, they believed the genuine or "deserving" poor would benefit, as less relief was dissipated on professional beggars exploiting the insularity of particular agencies. If each agency, maintained the C.O.S., pursued its own specialized functions there would be a drastic reduction in overlapping and waste, and more energy would be available to help people in the "ascent to the independent life".[1]

The acknowledged purposes and ways of working of any one social agency can together be called the function of that agency. This notion was inherited by later caseworkers whether they were employed in an agency whose primary function was social work or in an agency which had other purposes. In 1895, when almoners were first used in the hospitals, they saw their objectives clearly in terms of the institution to which they were "attached":

1. To prevent abuse of the hospital by persons able to pay for medical treatment.

2. To refer patients already in receipt of parish relief, and such as are destitute, to the Poor Law Authorities.

3. To recommend suitable persons to join Provident Dispensaries.

---

[1] "We, far more than our predecessors, have to make special efforts, devise new means that will facilitate the ascent to the independent life . . ." C. S. Loch, *A Great Ideal and Its Champion*, 1923, p. 54.

The importance of these objectives lies not in their negative quality, but in the clarity with which the almoner saw herself as helping to fulfil the objectives of the hospital. Later, the almoners undertook to humanize the institution in which they worked by giving the patient the time busy doctors could not spare. Similarly, early psychiatric social workers saw themselves as gathering data for the psychiatrist and facilitating his work with the patient by giving direct advice to the relatives.

The idea of serving an agency and securing its objectives is, thus, part of the history of social work, but what can it offer to the contemporary social worker? The notion of agency function has prevented casework from developing as a mere welfare trimming to existing services. This is an important viewpoint for workers in the child care field. In discussing the work of the child care officer, we are not discussing two entirely distinct elements, casework and the statutory obligations of the service. It is not as if statutory obligations were met and then casework practised if time allowed as a kind of welfare extra. Casework lies in the way in which these obligations are interpreted and fulfilled. In superintending foster homes, supervising adolescents and in other aspects of her work the child care officer will provide more effective service if she tries to understand the people and problems she meets, if she uses the function of her agency, and if she makes use of knowledge, skill and professional relationship. In other words, if she practises casework.

But how can the function of the agency be used? It can be used to help both client and caseworker concentrate their efforts at working on particular problems. Thus, a worker visiting foster parents by the fact of working for a children's department is primarily concerned with the child. The personal problems of the foster parents may well be pressing, but she will be involved with these only insofar as they affect the child. This is a valuable focus for her work and could be a support for the foster parents. The child care officer, they could say, has not therapeutic responsibility for us and the child, but comes to help us help the child. This kind of focus may prevent unhelpful expectations and the dissipation of energy in the attempted realization of numerous and unrealistic goals. In this country, however, a conscious study of agency function and its use in casework has paradoxically developed only since the present emphasis in casework training was laid on the elements common to casework no matter in what setting it is practised.

Caseworkers would now acknowledge that the sense of agency function should be communicated to the client. The client's co-operation in attempts to solve his problem can hardly be expected if he is not helped to see the purpose of the agency represented by the social worker and its general ways of working. The function of an agency is conveyed partly by simple explanation, but also by the worker's ease with administrative procedures and her confidence in the relevance and helpfulness of her questions in assessing the client's need for, and ability to use, a particular service. The importance now placed on conveying an idea of agency function to the client represents an important change in casework. For the C.O.S., particularly in its early days, the co-operation of the client was not actively sought in the process of giving help. Clients, it is true, might be classified as co-operative or non-co-operative, but this was based on their willingness or otherwise to answer the questions put to them. The purposes of the social worker in putting such questions or in holding the interview were not to be shared with the applicant. As a contributor to the *Charity Organization Reporter* wrote in 1881,

> "it would be difficult to overestimate the value of the first *scrutiny*, the first conversation . . . then how much is often gleaned by encouraging the applicants to talk! How much they will sometimes tell us of the points *we* want to know before they have any idea *that the information will serve our turn* . . ." [my italics].[1]

Work on Cases Governed by Certain Principles

"Principles" in casework are nearly always discussed in terms of values, whether these are ethical (*e.g.* respect for the unique value of the individual), political (*e.g.* the view that casework is somehow synonymous with democracy) or professional (*e.g.* the value of professional secrecy). The importance of such values, whether they are highly generalized or more directly tied to ends and means, is not disputed even though in this as in other aspects of casework their analysis has hardly begun and their exact significance remains unknown. In this chapter emphasis is placed rather on what might be described as technical principles and of these perhaps the most

---

[1] Graham, J. A. D., *Charity Organization Reporter*, February 24th, 1881.

crucial is that help should be offered on the basis of as precise an understanding as possible of the client's problems.

The element of casework to be discussed in this section has been called at different times in the history of casework, investigation, diagnosis, and appraisal. These terms refer to processes with different objectives, but they share a common reference to a close attention to an individual's particular needs. Prior to the advent of the C.O.S., relief work did not have the understanding of the individual among its objectives. Obviously there were enlightened individuals (*e.g.* Chalmers) and the occasional advanced agency (*e.g.* the Jewish Board of Guardians) who sought to give personal and perceptive relief to those in distress. The general attitude, however, in most agencies and amongst the general public was to dispense charity as an obligation that did not involve more than a gift to a beggar or a contribution to the expressed need of an applicant. The C.O.S. advocated closer inquiry into each application for help, and an end to mere indiscriminate almsgiving. They insisted that every application for help should be investigated fully with a close regard for the individual character, circumstances and responsibilities of each applicant. As the Annual Report of 1896/7 stated:—

> "Taking pains to go into each individual case shows us the great mistake is to give way to generalizing. No one who has worked on our lines for a lengthened period would say 'A drunkard cannot be helped' or 'All begging letter writers are impostors'; it is true this is difficult, and generally help is impossible but it is worthwhile looking into each case, or we may lose a good opportunity."

The emphasis placed on investigation can be illustrated by the first quotation that heads this chapter. What is advocated there is the elucidation of factors specific to a particular individual or family. Once such factors had been discovered a plan of help could be put into operation. Such a procedure appears reasonable, but in practice the C.O.S. had inadequate means to accomplish their ends and an unreal expectation of what they might achieve. To discover "causes, often more potent and less obvious, which lie in the character, habits and health of the family itself", they could use as sources of information only references of character, reports from other social agencies, and the applicant's own account. Such information was interpreted by the C.O.S. workers in the light of their own impressions and judged by their views on social duty.

These means appear even more inadequate when it is realized that these early caseworkers aimed to have investigation fully completed before any "treatment" was attempted. They saw themselves as casting a net over wide areas in the attempt to discover that one fact which would prove the key to the whole case. This attitude to a particular all-important fact is evident in the following comment on casework enquiry:

> "suddenly he (the applicant) gives an answer that throws a ray of light into the case, for it shows that years ago he did some other kind of work or that he has some connection in the country and might possibly migrate, or that there is some friend or relation who, though tired of giving aid that is soon used up and leads to no permanent benefit, might join in some larger scheme for the applicant's new start in life."[1]

It would be recognized today that it is extremely rare for the discovery of any single fact to make such a difference to the conduct of a case. What are usually of greater significance are the patterns of fact and the individual's own feelings about them.

Since the early twentieth century investigation has undergone at least two important changes. Social workers have given much closer attention to the individual's own account and systematically collected from him and his relatives a social history. Secondly, social workers have found that they can give more effective service if the distinction between "investigation" and "treatment" is not rigidly observed in actual conduct towards a client.

The social history, or the attempt to describe the significant events and relationships of the past in order to understand the client's present problem, was one of the major results of the influence of psychology which began to be felt in social work around 1920. The fact that at this time social workers began to look to psychology because of the difficulties they encountered in their casework is one of the most important changes in the history of social work. Other aspects of this change will be considered later, but one of the results of collaboration with psychologists and psychiatrists was undoubtedly an emphasis on the historical approach to a client's problem. This emphasis was most noticeable in psychiatric social work in both the child guidance and adult fields.

Fairly soon after the establishment of their training (1929)

---

[1] Laurence, K. L., "The Importance of Good Casework," *C.O.S. Occasional Papers* 25, Fourth Series, 1912.

psychiatric social workers began to see the social history in the context of the developing relationship between client and caseworker. Ashdown in 1936 recorded her opinion that the psychiatric social worker may in certain circumstances

"have to respect, even to applaud, the informant's reserve ... The psychiatric social worker must here shoulder her professional responsibilities and, even if it means foregoing the approbation of the psychiatrist, regard with some suspicion her natural desire to produce a 'good' social history."[1]

Psychiatric social workers also saw that the most informative material presented by the client was to be found not so much in a full, detailed history, but in the ways in which he responded to the caseworker at the time of the interview. In other words, an appraisal may be based less on a detailed knowledge of a client's past and more on an imaginative understanding of the wishes and fears he expresses in the present.

"Diagnosis must take account of family history insofar as this comes out through the parents' need to stress this or that trend in family relationships, but far more than in the facts of such a history, significance is seen in the parents' feelings about the facts, and the feeling attitudes of both child and parents as expressed in the behaviour responses to each other and to the therapist, be this psychiatrist or social worker."[2]

It is helpful in present-day practice to see these two approaches, the collection of historical material and the understanding of the forces at work in the present, as complementary rather than mutually exclusive. Certainly, in the child care field the worker will need to use both. Yet it is important to see that historical material is in fact both obtained and used. For example, Britton has drawn attention to the way in which the very process of collecting a social history may help a mother to see her child as a whole person for the first time.[3] Similarly, a good history taken when a child first comes into care may prove of considerable use when in later years the child has to be helped, perhaps by another child care officer, to piece together his past in order to understand what kind of person he is.

Seeing the process of investigation as part of a beginning relationship, helps to indicate the means by which this investigation is

[1] Ashdown, M., *The Role of the Psychiatric Social Worker*, 1936.
[2] Cosens, M., *Psychiatric Social Work and the Family*, 1932.
[3] Britton, C., "Child Care", in *Social Casework in Great Britain*, ed. Morris, C., 1951, p. 180.

2

carried out. In the early days of the C.O.S. considerable use was made of direct questioning and the applicant was given the rather passive role of informant. In such a situation it was easy for communication to break down and for cases to be dismissed because of "false statements". Helen Bosanquet at the turn of the century published *An Apology for False Statements* which as a sensitive appraisal of the difficulties of communication between caseworker and applicant could be read with profit today.

> "The fact which guides his statements, round which they all gather, and to which they will conform is the very engrossing one that he wants help and wants it with an intensity which dominates all minor interests to a degree inconceivable to an outsider; and his one endeavour is to bring this fact as clearly before the mind of the hearer as it is before his own. We, meanwhile, have accepted that aspect of the fact (though probably inadequately), and are trying to get at another which is absolutely uninteresting to our patient, which probably does not exist for him".[1]

This viewpoint does not seem to have influenced practice at the time, but this should not prevent recognition of its value for the present. Similarly, some caseworkers at the beginning of this century recognized that the manner in which investigation was made could be of benefit to the "treatment" of the case, though again this was probably not widely reflected in practice. Holman, for example, observed in 1912 that

> "it is above all things necessary that the patient, if we may so call the one to be helped, should take a leading, intelligent and active part in the process if his self-dependence and self-respect are to be maintained and improved ... This is the justification and aim of the questions which are asked."[2]

It has been suggested by contemporary critics of social work, like Wootton, that the caseworker's attempt to "understand" is a god-like presumption and that the clients of most social work should be helped only with the problems they explicitly present. The author has discussed these views elsewhere.[3] Here it will be sufficient to state that what caseworkers are claiming is not the possession of a key to the mysteries of life, but the opportunity to grope towards a

---

[1] Bosanquet, H., *The Standard of Life*, 1898, p. 189.
[2] Holman, J., "Restatement of First Principles of C.O.S. Work", *Charity Organization Review*, July, 1912.
[3] Timms, N., "On Wootton's Image of the Social Worker", *Social Work*, July, 1961.

precise understanding of their clients' problems and their meaning for them. This understanding is itself helpful to the client and it is the basis of effective help in the future. Caseworkers have attempted to understand because simple straightforward practical help has not always proved sufficient or even partially effective and because clients have asked for other kinds of help, sometimes explicitly, often implicitly.

In this commentary on the caseworker's attempt to understand the person needing help a brief outline has been given of the main developments since the beginning of the C.O.S. The major change can be seen as a movement from "investigation" through "diagnosis" to what might be termed "appraisal". The caseworkers of the C.O.S. began by investigating to discover fraud and imposture, but gradually they tried to ascertain not should this person be helped, but how could the caseworker help. The caseworker, however, could interpret his findings only in the same way as the ordinary citizen. Today caseworkers have a similar aim, but they interpret their findings in the light of psychological findings and they secure a different kind of information by fostering the co-operation of the client and by a close attention to the details of their mutual communication in the present.

Knowledge

A necessary preliminary to any discussion of "knowledge" in connection with casework is the recognition that no body of casework knowledge exists. Such an affirmation needs, however, immediate qualification, since it is based on a fairly firm view of what constitutes "a body of knowledge". We have no casework knowledge in the form of hypotheses that have been adequately formulated and put to tests which may be regarded as crucial. Yet the position is not as bleak as critics would have us believe. Caseworkers have had to rely from the early days of their profession on knowledge at every level of generality and at different stages of development. They have had to act when little knowledge was available.

From its early days, however, the C.O.S. was not content with dealing with cases on a simple practical basis. The work of the society was informed by what were thought to be "scientific" laws. C. S. Loch, secretary of the C.O.S. for many years, thought and wrote of these laws as eternal and unchangeable; they had to be discovered and conformed with if any progress was to be achieved. This view of scientific laws as edicts to be obeyed undoubtedly influenced the atitudes of early caseworkers. Yet caseworkers were encouraged also, spasmodically and, as we shall see, not always single-mindedly, to respond to the individuality of the applicant. Faced with the task of attempting such response, caseworkers looked for help to two sources—"sociological" and psychological knowledge.

At the turn of the century C. S. Loch was encouraging the caseworker "to know his district" and Helen Bosanquet wrote in 1899:—

> "Nothing but an intimate knowledge of the conditions under which our poorer neighbours live can give us true sympathy with their lives and enable us to define where their real difficulties lie; and one, if not the only way of getting this knowledge and wide sympathy is to set ourselves to a careful study of the district in which we desire to work— a study not only of the people themselves, but also of the local institutions and customs which do so much to make people what they are, and to which it is due that a district can be worked, not as a chaotic agglomeration of atoms, but as an organic whole."[1]

Yet caseworkers failed to develop social knowledge from their strategic positions. From time to time they called attention to the valuable material locked away in their case files, but the vocabulary they had at hand to describe people and situations continued to be that of ordinary moralizing and fleeting impression.

This insight into the importance of a knowledge of local conditions and the effect of differences of standard between classes remained undeveloped, and it is only now that social workers are once again considering the sociological knowledge they might use to understand their clients. There is at present in both England and America a considerable emphasis on "putting the *social* back into social work". That this emphasis is made as much by practitioners as by critics appears to be unrealized by the critics. Part of this emphasis is certainly ideological, part is extremely vague; some of it may be important. The ideological element comes from opposition to psycho-analysis, and is often accompanied by the doubtful assertion that psycho-analysis has in fact dominated casework since 1930. What requires investigation is the specific contribution that can be expected from sociological knowledge to the understanding and help of troubled people.

[1] Bosanquet, H., *Rich and Poor*, 1899, p. 6.

It would seem that there are two kinds of contribution that can be expected from this source—knowledge of present-day society and concepts which help us to describe and understand behaviour.

In terms of substantive knowledge, we have studies of families in different areas and in different social classes.[1] Some of these studies themselves show how difficult it is to observe the habits and behaviour of people in other social classes without obtruding one's own social class values.[2] Yet their cumulative effect has been to turn our attention to differences in cultural values and behaviour, and to the importance of bearing these in mind when we attempt to communicate with other people. A neglected area here is the relationships between work and the family, but this is perhaps part of the wider neglect in social work of *fathers*. Another area in which we can expect useful knowledge is that of social class. American studies show an interesting relationship between this and kinds of mental illness, and types of treatment.[3] In the social services the unskilled working class are dealt with very frequently, and the important repercussions on its members of cumulative treatment *as* the lowest in society are often neglected. Of sociological concepts, the most used in casework at the moment is that of "role". This is useful for differentiating aspects of a person's behaviour, feeling and ideas, and for linking them in a meaningful way to those of other significant people in his environment. Role refers to the behaviour expected in any social position, to the rewards, duties and attitudes considered appropriate to that position. Thus, a person in the social position of father is expected to behave in certain ways, to maintain a certain standard of child care, and he is entitled to look for the affection of his children. If he does not maintain the standards he may be said to fail in the role of father, if he does not receive his children's love, he may feel himself that he has failed *as* a father.

[1] *E.g.* Dennis, N., and others, *Coal is our Life*, 1956. Young, M., and Willmott, P., *Family and Kinship in East London*, 1957. Kerr, M., *The People of Ship Street*, 1958. Willmott, P., and Young, M., *Family and Class in a London Suburb*, 1960.

[2] *E.g.* Dennis *et al.* in their study of a mining community seem to judge methods of child rearing by essentially middle-class standards. They remark that love "does not manifest itself in a serious and detailed consideration of the development and problems of each child and a plan of action to bring up the child", p. 232. Why should it?

[3] See, *e.g.*, Hollingshead, A. B., and Redlich, M. D., "Social Class and Mental Illness", Gursllin, O., Hunt, R. G., and Roach, J. L., "Social Class, Mental Hygiene and Psychiatric Practice", *Social Service Review*, Vol. XXXIII, No. 3, September, 1959.

Psychology has had some place in social casework from soon after the beginning of the C.O.S., but the systematic uses of psychology obviously waited upon the development of the discipline itself. Workers like Octavia Hill were concerned about the wishes, desires and feelings of individual applicants, but they had little knowledge to guide their intimations. They reacted, successfully or otherwise, to the personalities before them, relying on their own intuitive feelings and on moral judgment. Gradually, caseworkers came to look to psychology for help in understanding their clients. This search for help seems to have began about the 1920's and was undertaken by caseworkers faced with urgent problems in the field. It started largely in the area of delinquency treatment and research and it began and has developed largely in response to practical necessity.

In 1918, Burt published the first brief but systematic statement of the relationship between social casework and psychology. He maintained—and many social workers have since echoed his remarks—that a great part of psychology was not of direct use to social work, but suggested that the psychology of individual differences was useful. He stressed the importance of attempting to understand the emotions of the applicant:

> "Among the poor . . . we are too ready to put down illogical peculiarities to deliberate obstinacy or deceitfulness, or to wanton stupidity and ignorance; whereas most frequently they are neither conscious in character nor intellectual in origin."[1]

In this way he indicated the two areas in which psychology was to have a most powerful influence—the emotional aspects, and the unconscious origins, of human behaviour.

It is in this respect that a particular branch of psychology, psycho-analysis, has had most beneficial influence. Again, this is a gradual development, often seen in piecemeal borrowing rather than wholesale incorporation. The first suggestion in the literature that psycho-analysis might prove useful to caseworkers was made in 1927.[2] The writer suggested that technically casework might benefit from considering some aspects of Jung's approach. In particular he mentioned the magic solutions that Jung's patients often seemed to

---

[1] Burt, C., "Individual Psychology and Social Work", *Charity Organization Review*, January, and June 1918.

[2] Wellwisher, "Lessons from Jung about Casework", *Charity Organization Quarterly* January, 1927.

expect, the difficulties of communication, and the value of personal influence. These ideas would now be recognized as some of the commonplaces of casework, but their suggested application to casework at that time came as something of a surprise—not least to Jung himself.[1] From the early thirties, however, there is increasing indication of the extent to which caseworkers—mainly those in psychiatric social work—are attempting to use psycho-analytic concepts.

The use of such concepts is sometimes criticized today as so much would-be impressive paraphernalia, having relevance to the problems of neither caseworker nor client. In a brief introduction no extended discussion of this topic is possible; the usefulness of some psycho-analytic concepts to casework may be judged from the following chapters. It is, however, worth observing at this point that talk of the psycho-analytic influences on casework frequently fails to specify exactly which aspects of psycho-analysis are thought to be influential or useful. Caseworkers appear to have made use of several different aspects.

They have certainly approached the task of understanding present behaviour by examining the past and the way it is reactivated in the present. They have been helped by the notion of ambivalence, the idea that feelings are usually compounded of negative and positive elements. This has led some of them to dwell too exclusively on the latent hostility of clients to the worker and to family members, but at least the presence of hostility has been recognized, and some of its functions appreciated. Caseworkers have learned about some of the ways in which people avoid painful problems. For example, we can assume they do not exist (denial), we can make other people express and carry the problems for us (projection), and so on. Caseworkers have profited, too, from using some of the explanatory theories of psycho-analysis such as the theory of the oedipus complex. This theory states that in the course of psychological development boys and girls become conscious at an early age of themselves as separate sexual persons and express an unconscious desire for an exclusive relationship with the parent of the opposite sex. This desire has strong unconscious sexual elements and demands the possession of the parent concerned. It results in

[1] Jung in a letter published in the *Charity Organization Quarterly*, April, 1927, expressed surprised gratification that his theories were thought of use in social work.

rivalry with the parent of the same sex and can be said to be resolved when the child has successfully identified with this same parent.

This is an extremely condensed set of examples of the different elements of psycho-analysis that have been found of use to case-workers. From such a set one conclusion at least can be drawn, psycho-analysis has been used not so much as a source of techniques, of ways of working, but of ways of increasing our understanding of people.

Skill in Human Relationships

One of the difficulties in any exposition of social casework is the apparently simple nature of what caseworkers do when they try to help people. They encourage people to talk, they listen sympa-thetically, they talk themselves. They give advice, perhaps, they encourage and support certain lines of action; they put people in touch with other agencies and inform them of resources or social provision or they recommend that their own agency should give money and material aid. Such a list of activities emphasizes two important aspects of casework, the caseworker's enabling encourage-ment of the activity of the client and his own activity, but it does not show that what is important is when and how these activities occur.

Take, for example, the problem of referral to another agency. Here the caseworker is using his knowledge of the community resources available, but this can be used in a way that simply brings client and service into contact, with little understanding of their feelings about using the help offered, or imaginatively and sympathetically. Two short examples will illustrate this contrast:—

(a) *C.O.S. Case*, 1910
   "A mother is sent to the C.O.S. for convalescence. Her baby has to be placed away from her so that she can convalesce. A home visit is made and the visitor notes that the mother cannot get out of her head the death of a neighbour's child. Convalescence is arranged, but the mother returns before it is completed because she is worried about her baby."

(b) *An extract from a published case*, 1954
   "The wife of a man with an involutional depression was referred to me because he was convinced that while he stayed in hospital, she had insufficient money on which to live, and was therefore starving herself. This was of course part of his delusions, but had also some basis in fact, because, as he knew, his wife

refused to ask for assistance to supplement the National Insurance. She came to see me, and at once broke out into an indignant tirade about the officials of the National Assistance Board, who made people 'feel like beggars', saying that she would rather starve than apply to them for assistance. I knew that she had lived all her life in Rotherhithe, and probably had bitter memories of experiences with the old Poor Law, but I also knew that this could not be the whole story, since not everyone of her generation felt hostile towards the N.A.B. I only had to say:— 'You may have had unhappy experiences of asking for Assistance", and she was able to pour out a description of her deprived childhood in a docker's family, with a father frequently out of work and a proud mother who would not even apply for bread tickets for herself and her children when they were hungry. My client remembered how angry she used to be with her mother, and expressed as much indignation with her as with the N.A.B. I said practically nothing and gave no advice. When she left me, I did not know what she would do. But, she wrote to me next day to say that after thinking things over, she was going to the N.A.B. She had been able, presumably through being allowed to ventilate her feelings in an understanding atmosphere, to relate her present attitudes to the past and get things into focus."[1]

These two extracts illustrate a change in casework to a greater understanding of the fairly complex feelings people may have about taking help. A contemporary caseworker trying to help the mother in case (*a*) to use the offer of convalescence would probably attempt to ease the mother's fears for her own baby which are indirectly expressed in her feelings about the death of the neighbour's child. The offer of a general facility (a convalescence holiday) was clearly insufficient for this particular woman. In case (*b*) it is possible to see a relationship developing between the caseworker and his client. The importance of such a relationship has been emphasized in recent developments in casework and resolutely attacked by critics.

. Historically, the idea of relationship seems to have had a fitful development. In the early days of casework there was a tendency to split off the "relationship" elements (the friendships) from casework and give them to "the friendly visitor", who often had a purpose more diffuse than that of the worker dealing with applications for specific help. Dealing with cases was thought to involve the matter-of-fact approach, objectivity and impartiality. These were not the qualities of the friendly visitor. It was around 1900 that some sort of attempt was made, unsystematic and unsustained as it was, to

[1] Myers, E., "Inner and Outer Needs", *British Journal of Psychiatric Social Work*, October, 1954.

bring friendly visiting into the main stream of casework. As Pigou wrote in 1901:—

> "Since the problem of material distress is so largely one of character, it is clear that the exclusive employment of strict business principles can never be adequate for its solutions, but that the steady exercise of personal influence, of kindly counsel and sincere open friendship, is an integral part of all genuine charitable work."[1]

It is clear that many workers who gave evidence to the important C.O.S. Committee on Organization and Methods in 1908 were feeling towards ways in which friendly visiting could be given to cases in which the Committee had decided to give no material aid.

Undoubtedly relationships developed between caseworkers and clients and the outcome was sometimes beneficial. Yet progress in the use of such relationship was hindered by the fear of dependence. Caseworkers in the C.O.S. were anxious to close cases as soon as possible and hesitant about any systematic follow-up of cases because this might encourage further appeals for help. One witness to the C.O.S. Committee on Organization and Methods expressed this fear when she reported that as long as the friendly visitor calls, "they will keep on asking for assistance in certain cases . . . and that when the visiting stops they will pull themselves together"[2]

It is in psychiatric social work that the most significant developments occur in the use of the professional relationship. Caseworkers in this field encountered in their clients feelings and behaviour which could not be explained in terms of the present situation. They found themselves, for example, the object of considerable hostility in spite of sincere efforts to be helpful. Such inappropriate feeling "belonged" not to the present but the past; it had been transferred from feelings in earlier relationships with parents and brothers and sisters. Psychiatric social workers recognized such transference, but they were divided about the way in which it should be handled. Some wanted to avoid these feelings by concentrating on the present reality; others advocated interpretation of these feelings to the client insofar as they hindered the progress of treatment. The debate amongst psychiatric social workers was conducted in rather daunting terms, but what was of considerable importance for the future of casework was the emphasis placed on the relationship between

---

[1] Pigou, A. C., "Some Aspects of the Problem of Charity", in *The Heart of the Empire*, 1901.
[2] Evidence of Miss Jackson, p. 82.

client and caseworker as the main primary means of help and the beginning of understanding of the complex nature of this relationship. The relationship is important for several reasons. The way in which a client relates to the caseworker (*e.g.*, in a dependent manner which barely conceals anger) gives useful information about the sort of person he is, because relationships are the primary means by which a person seeks to achieve his objectives in life. They are also the primary means of help. A relationship with a helping person, however, is complex because clients are not always certain of what they want, do not always carry out plans, or follow the rules, and cannot always meet the demands of society or themselves. In other words feelings enter the situation and deflect purposes and disturb plans. Yet they do not enter in a random manner, they influence situations because, consciously or unconsciously, people are pursuing unacknowledged purposes, avoiding unexpressed fears and seeking unrecognized goals.

The concern with relationship in psychiatric social work was of a rather exclusive kind. Some kind of division grew up between those who used the relationship to show clients how they expressed their problems in the way they related to other people and those who perhaps felt only an inferior kind of practical social work was possible for them. Such a development ran counter to that "subtle sympathy" which Octavia Hill advocated (in the second quotation at the beginning of this chapter.) A subtle understanding of an individual client helps us to see that he is asking for and perhaps needs a certain kind of relationship with the social worker. This relationship may be explicitly directed to the development of his insight into his feelings and behaviour or to support and encouragement and advice with a view to maintaining the present situation. What matters is that the kind of help given is appropriate in the light of both the caseworker's understanding of the client's personality and of the function of the agency the worker represents.

In this chapter a condensed and abbreviated discussion of casework has concentrated on the elements of casework. The main elements have been identified as a first approximation, and these have been considered briefly in terms of history and of the present day. In the following chapters, the task of the caseworker in the Child Care Service will be seen in the context of particular problems

encountered by a caseworker who is part of an agency, who tries
to offer individualized service, based on knowledge of different
kinds and on the use of a professional relationship. It is expedient
at the present time to emphasize the understanding the caseworker
hopes to achieve and convey, rather than any specific techniques
for achieving her ends. It is still very difficult to specify what the
techniques of casework really are and so it may be more fruitful to
apply at present Freud's dictum, "I would advise you to set aside
your therapeutic ambitions and try to understand what is happening.
When you have done that, therapeutics will take care of itself." [1]

[1] Letter to van Ophuijsen quoted in Lennard, H. and Bernstein, A., *The Anatomy
of Psychotherapy*, 1960.

CHAPTER 2

ADMISSION TO CARE

IT is not only logic that suggests beginning a discussion of casework in the child care service at the stage of admission. The provision of social care for the deprived child did not begin with the Act of 1948, but several important features of present-day care are derived from it. Of these perhaps the most important is the realization of the significance and purpose of admission to care. Before 1948 and certainly in the great period of the history of the voluntary societies in the second half of the nineteenth century considerable thought was given to helping the child once he was admitted to care. It is only recently that we have appreciated the significance for the child's life in care of what happens around the time of admission. This time is important whether the child is committed to the care of the local authority by the courts or received into care under section 1 of the Children Act, 1948. First, however, particular attention will be paid to this second group of children.

The first section of the 1948 Act will probably be familiar to most readers of this book, but it is worth recalling its provision:

"Where it *appears* to a local authority with respect to a child in their area *appearing* to them to be under the age of seventeen—
  (a) that he has neither parent nor guardian or has been and remains abandoned by his parents or guardian or is lost; or
  (b) that his parents or guardian are, for the time being or permanently, prevented by reason of mental or bodily disease or infirmity or other incapacity *or any other circumstances* from providing for his proper accommodation, maintenance and upbringing; and
  (c) in either case, that the intervention of the local authority under this section *is necessary in the interests of the welfare of the child* it shall be the duty of the local authority to receive the child into their care under this section."

The words and phrases in (the author's) italics underline the primary importance placed on the appraisal of the child care officer. Within very wide boundaries the child care officer's judgment of a situation is crucial. This judgment is given more weight when we consider the importance attached by the Act to the early formation of plans best suited to meet the particular needs of the child. How can such plans be made unless the child care officer in collaboration with parents and others can provide a reasonably detailed account of the child's social history? Finally, the skill of the officer is taxed by the fact that the Act inaugurates a service available to parents on a temporary or permanent basis.

The child care officer is concerned at the stage of application with a decision about the giving or witholding of a service and with offering some help in making arrangements for alternative care. This is a difficult process to manage, and it seems that child care workers are often divided by what could be termed the "eligibility" or the "need" interpretations of their function. One report of a Children's Department states that

> "While the great majority of applications are quite genuine, the sugges-
> tion of an investigation does at times cause the parent applying to
> withdraw his or her request. In other cases investigation has revealed
> that the application was not wholly accurate, and there have been one
> or two deliberate attempts to mislead."[1]

Notions of "genuine" or "accurate" applications assume the importance of testing whether this person is eligible for the service rather than appraising his need. His application may be misleading but his need nonetheless pressing. The Children's Department is not a department of general child welfare and it has sometimes to seek legitimate protection from heavy pressure from parents and social agencies. Yet too exclusive an emphasis on eligibility may result in harm to the child through failure to investigate the problem in child care that is actually facing the parents at the time of application. This is not to suggest that the truth about an applica-tion is unimportant, but, recalling Mrs. Bosanquet's *Defence of False Statements*, we have to ask ourselves why the applicant gives a false story, what does he hope to achieve and why does he make the attempt. In other words we see his statements not as so much evidence, but as clues to a more clear view of his underlying problems. It is perhaps worth noting that child care officers sometimes use the criterion of "genuine" or "misleading" because it seems to offer a

---

[1] *The First Four Years*, A Report of the Children's Officer of the City of Birmingham, 1949–1953, p. 12.

fairly practical and reliable means by which applications may be judged. Situations are often so complex that any criterion appears better than the lengthy, troubled way of trying to understand what problems the applicant has and what he is attempting to do towards their solution.

The second problem involved in admission concerns the attitude of the child care worker to the part to be played by the Children's Department in the provision of family care for the child. The child care officer has to make a decision in each case, not rely on such general notions as "any family is better for a child than separation". Considerable attention has, of course, been given to the possibly traumatic effects of separation on the infant and young child. Bowlby[1] has familiarized us with the general drift, if not the details, of the work of Spitz on the effects of hospitalization and that of Goldfarb, which is, perhaps, of particular interest to child care workers since several of his studies compared behaviour in groups of children raised in institutions and in foster homes. Yet the research of Lewis[2] warns us that care should be exercised in identifying exactly what claims are being made by "separation" research. This research is sometimes taken to justify such attitudes as "do not break up homes" and "children are always better off with their families". The individual researches, of course, make no such assertion, but their collective message is sometimes vulgarized in terms such as these. It is, therefore, important to appreciate, not simply that some children are so neglected that they must be removed from home, but also that some are so vunerable to the pathological behaviour of their parents that a protective service must intervene. Some parents will not be capable of giving minimal care and must be helped to part with the general day-to-day management of their children. This, of course, is not to deny that children often come into care who might have profitably remained with their parents or relations.

The first principle that ought to govern an application for care is the necessity for full enquiry into the circumstances of the applicants. It is now accepted that to enquire by means of routine questions is not a fruitful method. The variety of reasons for an application is so great that no routine administrative interview could cover them.

[1] Bowlby, J., *Maternal Care and Mental Health*, 1952.
[2] Lewis, H., *Deprived Children*, 1954.

Parents are anxious for their children to be taken into care during an emergency for a mixture of reasons. Some have no conception of the problems that even temporary separation can create for young children. Of these some seem very naive indeed. One mother said:— "I told them . . . it would be a nice holiday like; plenty of toys and lots of other kids to play with and good rations thrown in . . . what a lark!" She has perhaps a very idealized picture of a Children's Home, a "land of plenty" unhampered by the economics of ordinary family life. Or was she in fact denying some personal experience of separation in her own life which was the reverse of "a nice holiday"? Only individual investigation would reveal an answer to this question. For another anxious mother local authority care is a safeguard:— "I'd feel happier knowing you were taking care of them—I'd know they weren't being knocked around." Another sees it as the guarantor of family unit:— "Lucy would have the two eldest but she couldn't manage more—she works, you know . . . but I'd rather they were kept together, I think they'd settle better." A father who had coped successfully for a week with his family approached the local authority to take his children into care for the remaining time his wife would be in hospital: "I can't go on like this, and it's not fair to the kids either—children need a woman around to get a square meal." For some parents an application for care is a reluctant last resort: "I've no family to take them, but I've managed to get David fixed up with his school friend—she's very nice (the mother) and doesn't mind, but I don't know where to turn for the girls."

These brief extracts illustrate the sort of feelings parents may express when they apply for their children to be taken into care, and emphasize the importance of individualized investigation. Obviously everyone would agree in principle with this necessity; what is less clear is the manner in which investigation should proceed and the areas it should encompass. Take, for example, the following fairly typical application:

Application I

Report from Child Care Officer:

> Mrs. M. called at the office to enquire if her two young children could be taken into care, whilst she is confined with a third baby. Mrs. M. will be admitted to a maternity hospital in approximately five weeks'

time. The child care officer told Mrs. M. she would require certain particulars from her to place before the Children's Officer before a decision could finally be given. Mrs. M. is 32 years old and her husband, an egg packer, is 36. They have a council house on S. estate. They have two children, both girls, Anne who is 7 and Doreen, 4. The officer asked Mrs. M. if she could not make arrangements with relatives or neighbours to look after the children whilst she is in hospital. Her own mother is dead and her husband's mother is at present suffering from acute arthritis and is literally cared for herself by her husband. Her only sister is living in Portsmouth and they have lost contact within the last three years—she hardly knows the children apart from snaps, etc. Her neighbours both go out to work and she has few friends in the district. She is a withdrawn woman, shy and diffident. Husband's family can't help; he was an only child.

The officer asked Mrs. M. if either of the children has been away from home before and she said not. Her mother had coped with Anne when Doreen was born but the latter was born at home and her mother moved in. The officer asked her how the children felt about the new baby—she said she hadn't spoken much about it "in case they asked too many questions". Could Mr. M. not care for the children if Doreen went into a day nursery? She said Mr. M. was good to her but felt she could not leave him to look after the children as he was not very domesticated and she liked them "nicely turned out". She said if the girls came into care would we keep them together and that she didn't want them in a foster home but in a "proper Children's Home". The child care officer asked her whether the children had many friends and would feel uprooted away from home. She said she "kept herself to herself" and so did they. The officer acquired the image of two reserved children. She tried to explain to Mrs. M. that she thought they would be fretful away from home and that if it could be managed it would be better to keep them in their familiar surroundings. Mrs. M. was very resistant and said she thought they would settle very well as they were "very sensible girls".

The child care officer then told Mrs. M. that if the children were taken into care her husband would be responsible for their maintenance and that his income would be assessed accordingly. She was worried about this and asked whether the charges were high as they were not "well off". She was told that it would obviously be much cheaper and better for the children to keep them at home and send Doreen to the day nursery. The officer then suggested that she should discuss the matter with her husband and let the department know if she still wished to make a firm application and in that event her case would be placed before the children's officer but no guarantee that the children would be taken into care could be given.

In this case it seems that the idea of agency function has not been sufficiently used to help Mrs. M. She is not given at the beginning of the interview any idea of the services that could be provided or of the conditions under which they are offered. She does not know, in short, what her answers will be measured against. The questions,

3

too, are put in a way that makes the agency appear grudging towards Mrs. M. No one would advocate giving applicants precisely what they ask for at the moment of request (except perhaps Wootton),[1] but the vaguely grudging attitude probably does not help Mrs. M. to identify her problem and review the ways in which it might be solved. In other words, the worker should see herself not as guarding precious resources that must be sparingly used, but as seeking to engage the parent in a joint discovery of the dimensions and meaning of the problem and of the means to its solution. One of the likely solutions in the eyes of the parent is for the child to be taken into care and it is essential that the conditions (financial and otherwise) are made clear fairly early in the contact.

Obviously, the child care worker wants information, but this should be attained in a way that helps Mrs. M. to see her problem more clearly. This is, in a sense, to respect her as a parent. It is important to credit parents with some feeling of responsibility for planning the disposal of their child and to say to them, implicitly, "It looks as if we want to know a great deal, but we know you will want to be sure the best solution is reached". In other words the way in which the enquiry is made has an important effect on the applicant's view of the agency and of the problem. A grudging, routine enquiry will not encourage applicants to explore the problem as parents.

Applicants often come—Mrs. M. is an example—with their minds made up that reception into care is the solution to their difficulty. This makes them resistant to looking at problem and solution again. Many applications in fact become arguments between two value systems, the child care officer stressing the likely bad effects of separation from home, the applicant almost having to deny this apparent obstacle to his plans. In such a situation neither is really communicating with the other. Communication might well have been more effectively established if the child care officer had indicated some sympathetic understanding of Mrs. M.'s predicament in so far as this was revealed—a shy and diffident person coming to

[1] Wootton has argued in "Social Science and Social Pathology" and in subsequent articles that to attempt to discover a person's "real" problem instead of dealing with his immediate request of the social agency smacks of omnipotence. It is, however, not omnipotent to help a person consider the implications of his request and how far it will help in the solution of his problem. If he is unsure of the nature of his problem it is both sensible and helpful to assist him in discovering more of its nature.

ask for help which, for a number of reasons, was not available from relatives or friends.

Questions, of course, play an essential part in the process of application. The worker in the case of Mrs. M., for instance, could have enquired (usefully perhaps) how Mrs. M. heard of the Department. It is often interesting to discover this, since it reveals the sort of information, real and imaginary, that the parents may have about the function and working methods of the Department. Similarly, when Mrs. M. in the interview said she did not want the children to go into a foster home, it would have been useful to enquire quite simply why she had this preference, what might happen to them in a foster home that would not happen in a Children's Home. This would have told the officer something of what Mrs. M. hoped to accomplish by putting the children in care instead of making an alternative arrangement. There are many other questions that may be asked in this case. The matter could not really be decided on the information received so far. It would be important, for example, to see Mr. M. not only to attempt to discover how far he is capable of looking after a home while his wife is away, but also simply to recognize that he has some part to play in discussions about the disposal of his children.

Even this fairly typical application, then, requires skill and time for its successful completion. Other applications may represent more complicated situations. This is so in the case of Mr. and Mrs. X. and Belinda.

Application II

Mr. X. called at the office enquiring if it would be possible to take his daughter into care. He said that she was the child of his first marriage and that he had three children by a subsequent marriage. His second wife has refused to care for Belinda, the child of his first marriage, any longer. According to Mr. X. Belinda has been very difficult to cope with since the death of his first wife when she was seven years old and her behaviour had continued to deteriorate since that time. She is now 13 and a "real headache". He had married his present wife when Belinda was 7½ years old and although the child refused to accept her at the time of his marriage he felt that "time, kindness, and understanding would bring her round". Mr. X. said that he realized there were "faults on both sides". His wife is an excellent mother to the three other children but was never enthusiastic about Belinda. The child antagonized her from the start by rebuffing her overtures, by disobedience and cheekiness. She tried at first, according to Mr. X., to be friendly with Belinda but the latter seemed to take advantage of her and became "very wilful". The last few years have seen sporadic outbursts of family rows increasing in number and momentum. Belinda refuses to accept the authority of Mrs. X. and leads the other children into mischief. Mr. X. claims that she has developed a talent for "needling Ma".

The worker asked him how *he* coped with his daughter but he tried to evade this question by saying he was working a major part of the time and saw little of her. The worker pressed the point and he said that he personally would like her to remain in the home if only she would stop her provocative behaviour. Belinda is uneven in her attitude towards him—recently she was ill with mumps and was affectionate and clinging, but when she was up and back at school she became a little derisive and adopted a "Couldn't care-less" attitude. Some weeks she is anxious to meet him on his way home from work and other weeks she can hardly bear to say hello when he arrives.

Mr. X. is anxious to know whether the office could take her into care until she is older and is more sensible. He feels that for the sake of all the family she should not remain at home any longer, even though somewhere he says, "I don't like to turn my own girl in".

The worker told Mr. X. she would like to see his wife and Belinda so that she could put the full details of his case before the Children's Officer and he suggested a call at any time. An appointment for the following week was made.

Home Visit:

Belinda was not home from school when the worker arrived but came in later. Mrs. X. was full of indignation saying she hoped the worker had come to make arrangements to remove Belinda. The worker said perhaps she would like to tell her about Belinda. After half an hour's declamation certain important points emerged.

1. Mrs. X. was insistent that Belinda is "just like her mother" ... "all looks and no go". Apparently the former Mrs. X. was a very attractive woman. According to Mrs. X. she was "a lazy doll".
2. Belinda is a nocturnal enuretic and Mrs. X. is very angry about this —says it is just "laziness and spite" and that Belinda is teaching her children "filthy habits".
3. Belinda has pilfered from Mrs. X. on three occasions recently. Mrs. X. was full of moral indignation but is worried about the effect on the younger children in "having a thief in the family".
4. Could think of nothing positive to say about Belinda at all. Relations are really acutely strained.
5. Complained that Mr. X. spoils Belinda and fails to control her. She feels competitive towards Belinda re Mr. X. and seems to feel that Belinda threatens her marriage by perpetuating the memory of his first wife. This seems basically the ground of her antagonism towards Belinda.

Despite Mrs. X's views on Belinda she is not a totally unsympathetic woman. Her own three children, Joan aged 4, Phillip aged 2 and the baby who is seven months seem normal and affectionate in their behaviour. Mrs. X. spoke of Phillip's agressiveness towards the baby critically but not uncomprehendingly saying, "Phillip's a nuisance with the baby—he'll poke him if he can . . . he hates not being the baby any more . . . he is always after baby's bottle so I give him one too now when I feed . . . it keeps him satisfied".

The worker suggested tentatively that Belinda might feel similarly pushed out by the younger child but Mrs. X. would not accept this. She said Belinda is not a "youngster" and is really very "hard". She thinks Belinda is old enough to understand that young children need a lot of attention but not Phillip—"He's really only a baby himself". She was so impatient with this suggestion that the worker did not proceed. The worker considered that emotionally she has shut the door on Belinda and cannot open it at this stage. She has rejected her and whether she feels guilty or not she blames the whole situation on Belinda. She is too involved to be objective.

The worker saw Belinda when she came in from school. She is a tall, tense, attractive child. The worker introduced herself saying she had been discussing with Mrs. X. how the office could help her as it was understood she was not feeling very settled and happy at the moment. She shrugged her shoulders and said nothing. Mrs. X. told her not to be so rude but the worker ignored the reception and said she had to leave but hoped that they could meet again. The worker did not wish to involve herself too directly with the child until a decision was reached about the office's policy in the matter. Personally, she felt that it would help Belinda to be accepted into care as she could not see Mrs. X. modifying her views or changing her attitude to the child.

In this case the task of the worker receiving the application is to engage Mr. X. and, later, other family members in working towards the identification and solution of the problem presented by Belinda's behaviour. Children's Departments do not have to search anxiously for clientele, but the way they deal with applications may well prevent other agencies or themselves later having to deal with a deteriorated problem.

The emphasis on helping Mr. and Mrs. X. and Belinda to begin working out what the problem is helps them not to feel that the problem and solution have been taken out of their hands. Mrs. X. may well need more encouragement to work on her problem because she sees the child care worker as the aid or obstacle to its obvious solution, removal of Belinda. Within this framework the worker needs to focus much less upon the compilation of a historical account of Belinda's life and more upon the difficulties and strains in the active present and the sort of solutions the family has tried previously. In trying to bring the parents to this kind of discussion the worker will have to clarify the objectives and ways of working of her agency. Frequently, contact between agency and client is unfruitful because it is assumed by the worker that the client knows what he is applying to, and for, and can readily appreciate the purpose of the worker's approach to him.

At some stage in the application procedure in this case the worker will have to decide how far Mr. and Mrs. X. can be helped to make contact with other social agencies who may be able to help them. The possibility of Child Guidance comes to mind at once. A decision on the suitability of referral depends to a large extent on how far the worker feels she has time and the reasonable opportunity to help Mr. and Mrs. X. to see that there may be possible solutions, than the one of removal on which they seem set. It seems that in this case the father is more likely to respond to the attempt to change his focus on the problem than the step-mother. Mrs. X. can find nothing positive to say about Belinda even after she has had the opportunity to express an amount of negative feeling. Her response to the worker's attempt to help her to use her own understanding of a similar situation (Phillip's attitude to the new arrival, the baby) is unproductive. It is arguable perhaps that this attempt was premature, but it did test how ready Mrs. X. was at the moment to use "insight" which she undoubtedly possessed.

Whatever decision is reached in this case it is essential that all the family members concerned participate in planning for the future. It is in this respect perhaps to be regretted that the officer did not involve Belinda more than she did by at least declaring something of her possible function in this situation. What must be avoided is the quick surrender to Mrs. X.'s pressure for removal. Instead Mr. and Mrs. X. should be encouraged to participate as responsible parents in planning, so that if Belinda is admitted to care it is not a hurried act of rejection, but an act in which there is implied something of a future for Belinda. The outcome of any plan for Belinda depends very much on the worker's skill in involving Mr. and Mrs. X. in present planning and discussion. This is an illustration of the importance for the future of what the child care worker does at the time of application (and admission).

Sometimes, of course, talking of plans seems somewhat optimistic in view of strongly negative parental attitudes accompanied by equally strong feelings on the part of the child. The case of John (14) illustrates this. His mother took him to the Child Guidance Clinic after he had become unmanageable on the death of his father. He has an elder brother Frank at the University who is highly regarded by his mother.

Application III

10.11.60. *Second visit of Child Care Officer to the Home, following decision to admit John after case discussion with the Child Guidance Clinic.*

On this visit much was repeated, but the worker found the atmosphere worse and the discussion was not so much on the theoretical level. John definitely showed a lot of resentment towards both Frank and his mother. Frank came home yesterday and found John still in bed when he should have been at school; he was rather nasty towards him and hit him. Frank has told John that he always takes the woman's side because women are weaker and need protecting!

In the crisis of a few weeks ago when Mrs. P. hit John on the head with the poker, Frank had given John a good telling off and again John accused him of not trying to understand. John accused his mother of being different towards him when the worker was not there. The worker was not sure whether things were much worse between them or if she was in fact seeing them acting more normally towards each other. John kept saying that he wouldn't mind going to a Children's Home if it wasn't for the fact that he felt his mother was trying to get rid of him, and if he went she would get her own way. Mrs. P. pointed out to him that it wouldn't be nice for her to live on her own, and the worker said that this was only a temporary arrangement, and the fact that his mother understood this was proof that she wanted him back eventually and that they were only trying to help solve, or at least alleviate, the present difficulties. The worker saw several examples of the way John could flare up when interrupted by his mother, or when he felt she wasn't trying to understand, and could see that things could easily get out of hand. John said he always had difficulty in expressing himself and would she please give him a chance to try, etc. At one stage John said: "Well you often say that I want to be put away in a lunatic asylum, don't you?" and Mrs. P. just looked at the floor. John then got quite heated and said, "Well, don't you—answer me!" and Mrs. P. only said "let's not embarrass Miss E. (Child Care Officer), she's here to help us", and John gave up in despair. John said to the worker: "If you could see the look on her face sometimes you'd know that she wants to get rid of me", and the worker replied that we all did and said things we didn't mean when angry, but John said that this was something he could feel.

The worker told the P.'s that a decision must be made this week and it was eventually decided that she should take John up to see the family group home he would go to if he were admitted.

18.11.60. Collected John and took him to the family group home. His mother tried to get him to wear a tie, but John said he got too hot round the neck. On the journey John talked quite a lot, mainly about his father, because they were travelling near to his old works. They also talked about cars and John told the worker about his father's lorry, etc. The visit to the family group home could have been very awkward but in fact went quite well. The worker asked Cyril and Ian (children

at the family group home) to talk to John in the dining-room for a
while. They then played some records and had a cup of tea. John
was impressed by the visit and the home, and told his mother so
afterwards.

John's uncle was in the house when they arrived back and they all
had a short discussion. Both Mrs. P. and John's uncle were putting a
great deal of pressure on him to say there and then that he would go
into a home. They pointed out to John that if he didn't come into
care and co-operate on this occasion, he would probably be committed
to care by the Court, either as the result of bad school attendance or as
being beyond his mother's control. John said he wouldn't necessarily
be taken to Court because of school attendance, but his mother
rejoined that the authorities were only being lenient at the moment
because the matter was in the hands of the Children's Department.
John, however, stuck out and said that he would decide by Monday,
and Mrs. P. said she would 'phone the worker some time Monday
lunch time.

29.11.60. (*After John's admission to the Home*)
The worker visited Mrs. P. Frank was at home again but soon went
off to see a football match. Mrs. P. said she had visited the family
group home on Sunday and had a talk with Miss Carr, who she said
was a "very sweet woman". Mrs. P. said she had found a distinct
improvement in John already, and had great hopes of this "period of
training" being a success. She said the foster mother in the Home had
asked if John might not stay at the family group home on Christmas
Day as they had a nice party, and Mrs. P. said she would leave that to
John. She said in any case she wouldn't be alone at Christmas as
Frank would be at home.

In this case the worker has the important task of helping both
mother and child to appreciate and begin to take hold of the
function of the Children's Department. This is not easy (particularly in the interview of 10.11.60), when the worker has to interpret
her function to two people who have a conflicting interest in the
situation. However, it is possible to see this also as an opportunity
for the officer to show that she can at least begin to see how difficult
things are for both mother and son and that she wants to help both.
To the mother she can express some sympathy for her feelings that
John has got out of control, that the situation is so much out of
hand that someone must be mad; this seems to Mrs. P. the only
way to account for it. To John the worker might try to convey some
understanding of the great anger he feels. It probably does not
help him to say that his mother does not mean her anger. He
knows she does and he knows he means to be angry also. What are
they both angry about? Do they feel the recent death of the father
as a desertion, which has left John with some feeling that he ought

to carry more responsibility for the mother, and the mother feeling inadequate to bring up this male child now in adolescence? What was the relationship between mother and son like *before* the father's death? These are questions that require an answer before the child care worker can more adequately understand the situation. Her growing understanding will help her to take some of the pressure of decision off John's shoulders. This decision is obviously of prime importance, but it is not sufficient to say that if he decides to go into care the problem of the case has been solved. What is crucial is the way in which he comes to this decision, how he is helped to see some of the consequences of his action and that he is shown that the adults do not want to rush or trick him into a decision.

As the child care officer explains the problem and conveys her growing understanding to both Mrs. P. and John she will show the mother, for example, that she does not have to think of John going away for training and that John does not have to feel "bad" or "mad" because he is away from home. It may be that the mother and John cannot be helped to understand their situation by the same worker. They may have such conflicting interests that they are suspicious of what they may see purely as the other's worker. The suggestion that two workers should be used in what may appear a rather lengthy process of exploration may seem unrealistic. This may be so, but in working with more than one family member it is only realistic to appreciate the limitations that may be imposed on the worker by the conflicting ways in which the members wish to use her. In such a situation, the worker can more easily find herself in unwilling co-operation with one family member than if a colleague was working with the other member and supplying some kind of corrective to her feelings and action.

So far consideration has been given to cases that might be received under section 1 of the Children Act, 1948, and no attention has been paid to cases committed to care by the courts. Such cases present the child care officer with problems different in some respects from those faced in other cases, even though there is some empirical evidence that the mode of admission may be largely accidental for any particular child. In the first place the child care officer's responsibility in the decision to "admit" or not is now carried by the court, though the officer may give the court a report on the child and his home. Secondly, committed children will probably not, as in the case of many Section I temporary cases, be admitted directly to foster homes without a period of "reception". The time and process of reception are of great importance and the Sixth Report of the Children's Department of the Home Office stated that "The establishment of proper reception facilities is the keystone of a local authority's child care arrangements".[1] In fact facilities for reception vary considerably from one authority to another. Some maintain reception homes with the facilities of qualified staff, use of psychiatrist, regular case conferences and full records. Others use general all-purpose homes, or make no provision at all. Some occasionally use the reception homes of other local authorities. The general picture varies, but the function of the child care officer remains constant. She must ensure that an accurate and full picture of the child is obtained from those who have most to do with his previous care. This picture will include facts about his development and an attempt to discern the characteristic ways in which he relates to people, especially his parents and siblings. It will help to show how far the observations of his behaviour at reception are to be trusted as an account of his usual reactions. It will, also, remain as a recorded account of the child's previous life, so that should the necessity arise in the future, the child care officer will know, and be able to help the child to know, something of his life before he came into care.

This is the task in so far as it concerns the child, a compilation of his social history and an account of his usual ways of handling stress and relating to people. But there are also his parents. Some children are committed to care because proceedings have been instituted by the parents; others are committed because of an offence and others because they have been neglected by their parents. All the parents of these different groups share problems about their failure as parents. It is easy for them to deal with these problems by denying they exist and acting as if the child was dead or by putting all the blame on to the local authority that has the care of this child. It is not difficult for the child care officer to collude with such attitudes, for example, by acting as if the parents were psychologically no longer parents. What happens at the stage of admission is important not only for children but also for parents. Increasingly children committed to care are being allowed to go

[1] Sixth Report on the Work of the Children's Department, 1951, p. 22.

home under supervision. The outcome of this is largely dictated by how the parents and children were treated at the time of admission into care. If the parents were treated as completely unfit, as simply not parents, the separation will mark them in a way that is not easily erased, and in a way that does nothing to help them think about the resumption of the care of their children sometime in the future.

> John (8) and Michael (6) and Jean L. (2) were committed to the care of the local authority in 1959 because of neglect. The father was fined and the mother placed on probation. She was ordered to reside at the Mayflower Salvation Army Training Home for young mothers. The case had been brought by the N.S.P.C.C., though the Children's Department had made two visits before the children were removed to see if anything could be done to prevent prosecution.
>
> The child care officer who had made these visits was in court when the children were committed. The mother shouted abuse at the magistrates and had to be removed. When the child care officer saw the mother she sat on a bench looking depressed and empty. The worker said she supposed Mrs. L. remembered her. Mrs. L. made no reply. The worker said that she wanted to explain . . . Mrs. L. flared up and shouted that there was no need to explain . . . she had lost her children; the — officials had taken them; she had thought the worker had called to help, but she was as bad as the rest. The child care officer said that she knew Mrs. L. was angry and perhaps she could call and see her when she felt more calm. She just wanted to tell her where the children would be and to explain about visiting. It was not the Children's Department who had prosecuted.

In this case the worker has to deal with Mrs. L. at a moment of very great stress. Her account of Mrs. L. sitting on the bench, depressed and empty, shows that she understood something of her feeling, and she might usefully have begun by showing that she was "in touch" with that feeling, instead of wondering if Mrs. L. remembered her. It would be natural in this situation to be somewhat afraid of Mrs. L., and this perhaps accounts for the worker's attempt to postpone the interview. It would be natural, too, to feel uneasy when Mrs. L. equated the worker with the persecuting, depriving officials. Yet if the worker wished to differentiate herself from them she could perhaps have done this more effectively by showing she was different and she would show this by the way she communicated to Mrs. L. her perception of her feelings. Mrs. L. must surely feel so angry and in such a mess that she cannot go on to think about "arrangements" until these feelings have been recognized and to some extent, allayed. In this case the officer has to face, and help Mrs. L. to face, an accomplished fact, the removal of her children.

As Clare Britton has suggested the caseworker in the Child Care Service frequently has to work "backwards", explaining her actions after the event to both parents and child. This is one of the basic features of work in this setting.

> "Other caseworkers are called upon to help clients to work backwards over previous experiences in order to come to terms with the present, but unlike the child care worker they have not been the centre of the drama as the actual people who have acted."[1]

In "working backwards" the child care officer has not only to make her own action at that time understandable, but also to help the parents look to and work for some kind of future, either with or without their children. In the case of Mrs. L. of course, this is a distant aim, but a beginning can be made if she is seen and treated as a mother who has had her children removed, and who feels guilty at her own negligence and angry because she cannot face this or her own sorrow.

The children come into care by voluntary agreement or by court order. They may spend some time in a reception home, be boarded out directly with foster parents according to a pre-arranged plan, and remain in care for a long or short period. These are some of the possible variable factors in any one admission. Is it meaningless in the face of such variety to talk of the task of the child care officer at the stage of admission? Obviously different administrative arrangements have some effect on the officer's work. Basically, however, she is concerned with discovering the history and present functioning of the child so that plans can be made for his care in a way that is as precisely as possible related to his needs. Whether the child's stay is long or short, the worker's knowledge not only helps to form a plan but also assists the officer and others in its execution. The short-stay foster mother needs to know about the child's likely reaction to separation, to strangers and to change as much as the staff in a Children's Home require this knowledge. Such knowledge is particular to each child and can best be gathered as part of a social history. Equally important, however, is the way such information is obtained and this is part of the child care worker's whole attitude to parents, whether they are the parents of

---

[1] Britton, C., "Case Conference", *op cit.*, p. (v), *ante.*

committed children or of short-stay children. Finally, for both child and parent the process of admission is important. Is this a hurried introduction of the child to the Home or foster parents, a perfunctory word with angry parents after a court hearing? Or is it a more careful introduction, a more secure explanation that sets what is happening now in the context of the past and of a possible future?

CHAPTER 3

CASEWORK WITH CHILDREN

"There is a certain type of client who creates special problems in the administration of social agencies and in the interviewing situation. This client seems totally unable to comprehend the function of a social agency. He frequently creates disorder and chaos in the waiting room: often he talks loudly and shrilly, demanding numerous attentions, and has been known to look boldly over the shoulder of a typist as she transcribes confidential reports. In the initial interview with the caseworker, this client states more or less positively that he has no problem and he does not know why he has come to the agency. Further difficulties are encountered when it appears that he cannot sit in a chair for more than five minutes. He tends to concentrate on irrelevant matters like the operation of the Venetian blinds . . . The client has neither marital problems nor employment problems . . . The sex of the client may be male or female. The age is roughly five to fifteen. What are we to do with him?"

S. FRAIBURG[1]

THIS quotation seems to express with brevity and charm some of the absurdity or challenge we may feel at the prospect of offering casework to children. Indeed the notion of the child as a possible client is a comparatively recent development in casework in this country, and it is of interest to trace briefly some of the main changes in casework attitudes to children.

Reformers in the middle of the nineteenth century were anxious to compensate children without families of their own and in some of the better institutions the aim of re-creating family life was accepted. Mary Carpenter, for example, said of the child who lacked proper parental care that "He must have his affections called forth by the obvious personal interest felt in his own individual well-being by those around him; he must, in short, be placed in a

[1] "Some Aspects of Casework with Children", *Social Casework*, November and December, 1952.

38

family".[1] In work with parents of children in their own homes, however, this idealization of the family emphasized the status and responsibilities of parents, and children were hardly seen, let alone heard. This attitude persisted well into the present century. Caseworkers might talk of offering help to "the family as a whole", but their actions showed that they were concerned with establishing households in economic independence. Thus, in 1933 casework with a family resulted in the following plan to enable

> "the mother to regain her strength and lead her own life with her children, while preparing the children to stand on their own feet . . . It was possible to arrange for the elder girl, who was anxious to go into service, to be sent to a domestic training school, where she will be thoroughly equipped to earn her own living. The younger girl was sent to a suitable home until she should be old enough for training, while provisional arrangements were made to send the boy away to school should it prove necessary."[2]

Even when direct help in placing a child was requested, the child was not seen as a "client" in his own right, and the casework seems to be evaluated entirely by its effect on the adults. In 1928, the case of a child placed in a foster home by a family casework agency, is described as "bad" because the *father's* character has not been improved by association with the agency.[3] This was the kind of situation in which caseworkers could profitably have asked, who was the client?

A gradual change in this kind of attitude began with the introduction into England of the Mental Hygiene Movement. Caseworkers began to see themselves as interpreters to parents of the behaviour of their children. A published account of the case of a boy of ten, restless and attention-seeking at school, shows the worker in the first interview discussing educational methods and giving

> "instances of children, who, perhaps as a result of early deprivations, felt an exaggerated need to be in the limelight even when the consequences were always painful. Restlessness was instanced as drawing a great deal of attention and the worker even went so far as to ask whether Jimmy did not get more attention through his restlessness than for anything else."[4]

This stage of casework, which characterized much early child

---

[1] Mary Carpenter, *Juvenile Delinquents, their Condition and Treatment*, 1853, p. 298.
[2] Charity Organization Society Annual Report, Deptford District, 1933/4.
[3] Case quoted in Timms, N., "Social Work in Action—A Historical Study" (1887–1937), *Case Conference*, May, 1961.
[4] Cosens, M., *Psychiatric Social Work and the Family II—Illustrative Material*, 1932.

guidance work, assumed perhaps that a straightforward explanation would always help parents, but it recognized a bond between parent and child which was emotional and not economic in character. This relationship became the centre of the caseworker's attention, and the claim was made that children could not be treated unless their parents were also helped at the same time. This view of the limitations of a particular treatment approach often appeared in the form of an ideology which is still active in subtle ways in the child care field—no problem children, only problem parents. More recently, the notion of "inter-action" has received attention, and this is one of the most important developments in the field of social work. Coleman, Kris and Province,[1] for example, have presented four case studies in which the original relationship of the mother to the child, whether positive or negative, was influenced in the reverse direction by the growth of the child. They suggested that parental attitudes towards children are continuously influenced by the child's own growth and development and that there is a considerable adaptive element in parent-child relationships.

This kind of approach helps us to understand more clearly the forces at work in any given situation and to look on casework problems with some flexibility, feeling free to offer help to parent or child or both. Caseworkers in America have offered casework service to children for many years, but in England such practice has hardly begun. Is there anything in the principles and practice of this kind of casework that can be applied in the Child Care Service?

At a first glance it seems that a strong body of opinion inside and outside the Service would seem to question the usefulness of this development as far as child care workers are concerned. For example a recent study observed that

> "To the child, the caseworker's first responsibility is the provision, then, of a healing environment, while she herself does not give a primary relationship but rather represents the continuity in his life which the department tries to ensure, an assurance of safety, security and concern which will remain constant in a situation of change."[2]

This view optimistically neglects the tenuousness of the child's social environment and the frequency with which the child care officer is called on to help children change from one environment to another.

---

[1] Coleman, R. W., Kris, E., and Province, S., "The Study of Variations of Early Parental Attitudes", *Psychoanalytic Study of the Child*, Vol. VIII, 1953.
[2] Heywood, J. S., *op. cit.*, p. (v), *antc*, p. 182.

It obscures the different objectives child care workers have in different kinds of situation, and underrates the part played by their direct relationship with the child in securing these objectives. Effective casework help can be given to children by the child care workers to gain a number of essential objectives:

(i) in preparation for an experience, or in assimilating the experience if it has already taken place: such help may be a supplement to, or a substitute for, the help of parental figures; it could be called help with crucial events;

(ii) to engage in and maintain relationships; this could be called instrumental help;

(iii) at all times by the way the worker accepts people and is able to maintain contact with people who have different if not conflicting interests in the situation: help by demonstration.

Consider the following situations:—

(i) Jean (6) and Sandra (8). Previous arrangements for their care by relations have broken down because of the premature birth of their baby sister. Father has had to return to sea that day, but has told them they will be spending a day at the seaside with a nice lady. They have never been away from home before.

(ii) Beryl (8) and Jennifer (15) boarded out. Foster parents very attached to Beryl. They object to Jennnifer working in a factory and her association with her "coarse, vulgar father". Father has deserted mother and is cohabiting. Jennifer wishes to return home. Child care officer is in contact with father over this.

(iii) Gwen (8). Her mother has recently been admitted to mental hospital. Father deserted two years ago. She has been slowly introduced to prospective foster parents. On the way back from a week-end with them she asks about her mother and, in the course of talking, remarks how angry her mother used to become when she played out of her sight. She also wonders what she should call the foster mother; "Auntie Jennie" sounded funny.

These situations are typical of the work of the child care officer and they demand something more than the kindly adult who explains and acts, somehow or other, as "the constant element" in the child's changing life. A child care worker has a valuable role to play as the "link" between past and present, known and unknown, but she has to do more than demonstrate this by her physical attendance at moments of crisis. She becomes the trusted link for the child by the way she grasps the meaning of the situation to him, by the success of her attempts to give specific help. Are there principles of casework with children that can help her to do this?

4

Most of the characteristics of casework with children follow from the very obvious fact that the child is growing into adulthood. This involves a number of considerations—there are stages of development with particular problems and tasks and characteristic ways of behaviour; the child is at all times dependent on the parents or parental figures, though this dependence takes different forms at different stages; the child grows by distinguishing himself from the world and slowly ordering and managing his inner feelings so that he can act appropriately in the world. This series of statements is extremely compressed and the discussion that follows on child development will be concerned with its expansion and elucidation. But even the summary suggests that casework help to children depends upon a number of factors. In each case we should ask what is the problem facing this child at the moment and how can it be stated in terms of his own inner world and of his social relationship. What stage of development has he reached, since this will indicate some of the main positive and negative factors at work and something of our approach to him? Finally, we should know how much help he might expect from the important persons in his life, particularly, parents and parent figures, and how they are likely to respond to changes in his behaviour. To seek information on these areas may seem an exacting task, but there are sources of help to which the child care officer may look with some confidence.

Childhood Development

The games, the thought, the fantasy and the relationship of infants and children have been investigated, discussed and interpreted on so many levels in so many books that the separation of the helpful from the haphazard, the useful from the fatuous, is an almost impossible task. The problem of creating a unified set of theories that would describe and explain child development has only recently been faced[1] and we have made little advance towards a more exact formulation of the challenge presented. We still know very little about child development in terms of established theory.

Yet, as has so often been pointed out, the social worker has to act here and now and cannot wait upon the slow accumulation of knowledge. Workers in the child care field have to penetrate,

[1] See *Discussions on Child Development*, ed. Tanner and Inhelder, Four Vols., 1953-6.

understand and act in the world of childhood in a way that helps the child grow towards adult feeling and adult behaviour. Faced with this problem, on the one hand, and the mass of study and speculation, on the other, the child care officer may understandably seek refuge in believing that each case is distinct and individual and acting on a rather blind pragmatism. There is a fruitful alternative. We can usefully equip ourselves for entering the world of childhood by adopting the attitude of listening, not just to what the individual child is saying, but rather to what he is asking for. In other words we see his behaviour as attempting to communicate wishes and fears, hopes and dread, uncertainty and sureness. In attempting to appreciate what children are trying to tell us it is important to realize that the child's world is less surely anchored than the adult's and that his relationship to it is still being worked out. The child particularly the young child, relies to a considerable extent on magical thinking, especially in moments of stress—thinking *makes* things so *now*. The vocabulary of adults contains many references to time and to place, to order and stability. ("If you stay here for a little while, Mummy can get well and soon you'll all be together at home again".) For the child, however, ideas of sequence and restraint cannot be taken for granted; they require support and nurture.

In our attempts to understand what precisely a child is trying to ask for, we can use knowledge from three main sources: experience that has been felt, recalled and examined, knowledge of important theoretical concepts, and knowledge of stages of development.

By "experience" is meant active engagement in a living event. This may be direct, as in the case of playing with a two-year-old, or indirect, as in the case of reading some of the writings that attempt to describe the world of childhood. These writings are fairly extensive, but examples would include some of the descriptions of the impact of institutional and foster care on a child, such as Hitchman's *King of the Barbareens* or Vaizey's account of hospital life.[1] Fiction can be as stimulating to the imagination as autobiography and Golding's *Lord of the Flies*, for example, presents a vivid picture of a group of pre-adolescent boys. This brief reference to autobiography and novels cannot convey anything of the impact of reading them, but it is important to remark on this source of

[1] Vaizey, J., *Scenes from Institutional Life*, 1959.

possible new experience. We may have little certain knowledge about children, but any sensitizing experience in life or literature may increase awareness of the meaning of the communications of individual children.

This is not to deny or depreciate the value of theoretical concepts. These can direct our attention to important areas of feeling and behaviour, and important processes. The influence of events and relationships at the beginning of life, for example, helps to emphasize the value of the systematic collection of a social history. Yet the social history is not simply a record of facts that are past; in the life of the individual history repeats itself in varying ways in the present. Consequently, we collect historical information more effectively in the course of work in the present. As a problem emerges in the present we begin to ask of ourselves and others, how long has it been going on, has anything similar happened before, and if so what was done about it?

An example of the repetition of the past can be seen in the case of John aged 7.

> John has been in care since he was five. His mother went into a mental hospital soon after the birth of Moira; the father tried to keep the home together, but eventually deserted with the woman who was looking after John and Moira. John was placed in a foster home where there were no other children. He settled so well that it was decided to foster a second child, a boy of 6. Soon after he arrived John started to stay out late at night and to try to cause trouble between the foster parents, siding first with one and then the other.

This is certainly an instance of a child attempting to recreate the past and this aspect of childhood will be discussed later, but what should be noticed here is that as a result of past experiences he is extremely vulnerable in the present to anything that he might feel was the equivalent of the arrival of a sibling. Such an event presented him again with the problems of jealousy and of anger and also of fear that his new family might break up as had his old. It is probable that the child care officer already had sufficient historical material to understand the situation, but if she had not, it would have been helpful to her to begin collecting such material through examining the behaviour, feelings and problems manifested in the present.

It is helpful, also, to think in terms of the tasks of infancy and childhood. Perhaps the two most important are the establishment of a reasonably firm identity (I am myself and no other) and a fairly constant sense of worth (I am loved and can love). The sense of worth is established when the existence of good and bad within oneself is acknowledged and when it is possible, by and large, to feel confident that the good endures and is stronger than the bad, without having to deny the existence of the bad. Bowlby believes that this task is of the first importance in child care:

> "a principal criterion for judging the value of different methods of child care lies in the effects, beneficial or adverse, which they have on the child's developing capacity to regulate his conflict of love and hate and, through this, his capacity to experience in a healthy way his anxiety and guilt."[1]

To establish a sense of identity and worth is, of course, a long and difficult process. At any time in infancy, childhood or adolescence what has been achieved can soon be seriously endangered. To avoid such danger the personality evolves ways of dealing with internal and external problems which gradually become habitual; they may be seen as an individual's characteristic way of responding to stress. Take, for example, the internal discomfort of loving and hating the same person. Such discomfort may, of course, be created and sustained by separation from this important person and this discomfort will have to be managed in some way or another. One way of dealing with it, often seen in the work of child care, is by the recreation of the past, in either its painful or pleasant aspects. If the child can succeed in doing this he is reassured in a number of important ways. He is encouraged to feel that the situation is not completely out of hand because he has powerfully created the past again. He may feel that the recreation of an unpleasant past is an act of restitution for harm for which he feels responsible. He may feel that his present emotions are justified if he can create a past in which suffering was inflicted upon him. We can see the case of John above as illustrating each of these possibilities.

This way of dealing with problems is fairly developed and is used by children beyond the stage of infancy. Earlier ways of dealing with problems, internal or external, are predominantly splitting, introjection and projection. When an infant is faced with the problem of his own hating and loving and the threat to his good

[1] Bowlby, J., "Psycho-Analysis and Child Care", in *Psychoanalysis and Contemporary Thought*, ed. Sutherland, J., 1958, p. 35.

internal possessions by the bad frustrating aspects of his mother, he often "splits" the good and bad aspects of his mother and attempts to keep them separate. Dealing with the problem in this way makes the feelings of love and hate tolerable. Splitting can frequently be seen in children and adults. For example, the foster child who has a conflict of loyalty between her natural home and the foster home, and feels perhaps guilty at beginning to like the foster parents, may split the love/hate and make her own parents all bad and her foster parents all good, so that her present feelings towards both parties seem appropriate.

Introjection and projection are also important processes. Melanie Klein has shown that they characterize much of the early life of infancy, and continue as elements in adult life.[1] Introjection refers to the process whereby events and people, and aspects of people, which are external to the child are taken into the self and experienced as part of the inner world. John, for example, can be seen as having taken into himself the whole family problem of the past and to be asking by his behaviour "Am I deserted or deserter; am I like mother or father". Projection is a term that describes the opposite process. The foster mother who says that the child is restless whenever the child care officer comes, for example, may well be projecting her feelings of confusion or doubt or fear onto the child.

We have, so far, been illustrating some ideas and processes that might be of use in understanding children. We have concentrated on the problem of reconciling the good and the bad and some methods which infants and children may use, unconsciously, to solve the problem. This problem is certainly paramount in child care. It is also part of a crucial feature of childhood, the interaction of the inner and outer worlds. In every case the child care officer should ask herself what does the problem mean both in terms of the child's past and present relationships and of his own inner world.

There are two other aspects of childhood that must be discussed, the importance of parents in the child's life and the notion of stages of development. The mother–child relationship has occupied the attention of many psychologists, psychiatrists, social workers and others. Fathers are beginning to be appreciated, and a picture is emerging of the special roles each may play as the child develops.

[1] For a brief account of her views see Klein, M., *Our Adult World and its Roots in Infancy*, Tavistock Pamphlet No. 2, 1960.

The mother establishes the beginning of the child's growth by her love and physical care, the father represents the world outside the home. Both, however, are involved in the process whereby the child begins to share love without having to demand constantly the presence or exclusive attention of one parent. In sharing the love of father and mother the child begins to experience the difference between them and to establish his own sexual identification with the appropriate parent. These processes of sharing and of establishing sexual identity are part of what is commonly referred to as the Oedipus complex.

The fact that parents are important at all stages in the child's life, though in different ways and degrees, has some important implications for casework with the child.

The caseworker's relationship with the child, as I have said, must be based on recognition of the fact that he depends on parents or parental figures and that the help he receives through them is often-the most beneficial and lasting. One of the very few accounts of casework with a child published by an English writer demonstrates nicely the aim of working on a circumscribed problem, but totally neglects to mention why this help could not have been given by the parents.[1] Often, of course, because the worker has knowledge (either of the problem in general or of some particular aspect of past history) or because of her special position, outside the personalities facing the problem, she can and should supplement help from other sources. This needs, however, to be based on a clear assessment of the actual help that is otherwise available. This in its turn calls for a high order of skill.

In casework with adults we are used to clients who react retrospectively to past events connected with parents, but the child is experiencing his parents at the same time as he sees the caseworker. "His original objects, the parents, are actually in existence as love objects . . . between them and the child exist all the relationships of every-day existence."[2] This has two important implications— adults are seen as powerful by the child and the caseworker should always appreciate the child's dependence on his home. There should not be too striking a contrast between behaviour permitted at home and that allowed in the caseworker's presence. The child

[1] Lloyd, K., "Helping A Child Adapt to Stress: the Use of Ego-Psychology in Casework", *Social Service Review*, March, 1957.
[2] Freud, A., *Introduction to the Technique of Child Analysis*, 1928, p. 37

should not be given, in addition to his other difficulties, a problem of loyalty, and the caseworker should always consider the possible repercussions of intervention on the child-parent (or parental person) relationship. In undertaking direct work with children it is always important to consider the areas of behaviour in which parents or parental figures will be most able to co-operate with the caseworker. To proceed in the face of opposition, unacknowledged or patent, may nullify the task or even worsen the situation.

Finally, a brief reference must be made to the idea of stages of development. The notion of a series of clearly differentiated phases of growth and the gradual if uneven movement from one phase to the next, is open to serious criticism. Yet use of the idea encourages us to recognize differences between children not in terms of chronological age but of the emotional problems they are facing and the resources available to them. A useful attempt to describe stages of development has been made by Erikson.[1] He views the life of the individual as consisting of the Eight Stages of Man. He sees each marked by a main objective and characterized by what could be called an anti-objective, that is the sort of outcome that would characterize failure at that stage of development. Infancy is divided into three stages, each with its objective, (1) basic trust as opposed to mistrust; (2) autonomy as opposed to shame and doubt; (3) initiative versus guilt. The main problem of latency (4) (i.e., the period from the end of infancy to the beginning of adolescence) is seen as that of industry versus inferiority, while the task of adolescence (5) is seen as the establishment of a sense of identity as opposed to a scattered sense of self. This is a very bald summary of five of Erikson's Eight Stages, but the scheme helps us to think of stages of development not in terms of descriptive behaviour but of the main tasks of each period.

Skill and Objectives in Casework with Children

One aspect of casework to which perhaps insufficient attention has been given is that of communication. This certainly presents a problem in work with children (when important objectives may have to be accomplished in a car journey of an hour or less). Sydney, the heroine of Elizabeth Bowen's *The Hotel*, found herself in a cemetery with Cordelia, aged eleven. Cordelia remarks:

[1] Erikson, E. H., "Childhood and Society", *Imago*, Chapter VII.

" ' There is a rubbish heap at the back of the chapel. If you'd come with me I could show you?'

'What a horrid little ghoul you are!' Sydney said mechanically. She found that in actually dealing with children theories collapse and one must retreat on the conventions." (p. 138.)

In child care work neither theories nor conventions should intervene between the caseworker and the child. The theories should be seen as ways of illuminating what the child is trying to communicate, and of helping the caseworker communicate with the child.

In many of the records of casework with children, considerable emphasis is given to the participation of worker and child in some form of play activity. Sometimes it seems as if children are expected to "play out" their difficulties. This is an expectation which may lead to harm for the child and almost certainly disappointment for the worker. The child, for example, who is simply encouraged to bring more and more aggression to his play will become more and more anxious if this produces no therapeutic response and child psychotherapy is not the task of the caseworker. Rather, play can be seen as a way of communication which children find natural and relatively easy and through which they can be encouraged to refer obliquely to their problems. Communication is established by allowing and helping the child to discover the kind of person the caseworker is, and this often means letting the child form some kind of "relationship" with the caseworker's car or office. It is natural for the caseworker to suggest visits to a park, a zoo, to offer sweets, etc. (An English caseworker writing of work with a very inhibited 8-year-old in America: "I asked Brenda if she liked bubble gum and she said that she loved it, so I gave her a piece and I had a piece myself!") In other words, work with children, compared to work with adults, relies more on oblique reference to problems. We should attend in such work to the variety of ways in which children may be communicating with us, to the significance in terms of communication of drawings, stories, and other vehicles which can carry symbolic meaning.

But what is the purpose of casework with children? Talk of play activity and symbolic meaning and reference to America may suggest that some kind of play therapy with "deep" problems is envisaged. This reaction is perhaps partly due to the contemporary equation of "casework" with some kind of long-term therapy and the failure to see that it is neither length of treatment nor exclusive concern with emotional problems that distinguish casework. The objective of casework with children is to help in the solution of a problem. This requires three operations—the identification of the problem, consideration of its meaning and possible solutions, and action. The caseworker will help the child to deal with his problem in reality and to express and discuss his feelings instead of relying exclusively on denial, escape or regression. This does not mean an attempted exploration of the unconscious roots of the child's feelings, but the examination of feeling in connection with the problem. Without this exploration of feeling a real solution to the problem will not be found. At the same time, the caseworker should always bear in mind the stage of development reached by a child, and not stimulate a child to explore feelings beyond his power or his knowledge. For example, an inhibited 8-year-old asks the caseworker to draw. The caseworker asks what? "People," says the child; "people with clothes or without?" asks the caseworker. This question is stimulating to the child rather than helping her to sublimate her sexual curiosity. The child has really given no indication of the kind of people she is concerned with and the caseworker could more appropriately have asked "Men or women? Young or old?" and so on.

It is obvious that most of the examples above refer to particular incidents, but casework with children is not a question of the clever (even if correct) guess at what the child is feeling. It consists of the patient attempt to understand his problem, and to use knowledge and understanding directly and indirectly to help him to solve it. It is also obvious that the examples have been taken from children aged between 5 and 10, and in general, casework with children is usually concerned with this age range. (Adolescents are separately considered in another chapter.) Some writers speak of offering casework to help infants. Gordon, for example, suggests that, those "too young to be aware of and to communicate the specific nature of their concern, and too young to understand verbal explanations of what is happening, also need and can take some help from the caseworker".[1] This seems an extreme position, but it would probably be true to say that some casework can be attempted with the child of three, which would be something more than the

---

[1] Gordon, H., *Casework Services for Children*, 1956, p. 91.

generalized warmth appropriate in any adult's response to the infant.

I wish now to return to the case illustrations given above and to comment upon them and others in the light of the foregoing discussion of the aims and methods of casework with children.

(i) *Jean and Sandra* (p. 41, *ante*)

In this case the parent has avoided telling the children the truth of their situation because it would be painful and difficult. We, professionally detached from the child, have less excuse if we do the same. In this situation the children will feel lost and it is important to tell them where they are in relation to their parents (Daddy knows where you will be: Mummy will know or knows already) and where their parents are and why. It will also be helpful if the events of the present can be explained in relation to a plan (this is happening because . . .). In these ways the situation may take on some shape for the children, but this is something that may be hard for them to retain, so it may be advantageous to repeat the explanation at the end of the journey before the child care officer departs. It will also assist the children if they can see that their short stay will help their mother; this may "catch hold" of a purpose which will be a stand-by when the worker has gone. In explaining the kind of Home to which the children are going it may be useful to stress arrangements for schooling and the kinds of other children they will meet—this age-range shows considerable concern over attainment and group relationships. Explanation of the concrete details of the Home and its routine is helpful in two ways; it helps the children to envisage what the future may be like, but, more important, it helps them, when the worker has gone and they find the Home as she had foretold, to feel that there is order and shape in the world and adults who can be trusted and who know things.

All this may sound as if the worker does all the talking. This would obstruct the aim of helping the children to see their problem and express feelings about it. The worker who talks at length in the attempt to cheer a gloomy child, and the worker who relapses soon into bewildered silence, leave the child engulfed in his feelings of loss and betrayal. The worker may have to talk a great deal; the children may, for example, try to avoid the pain of the situation by becoming absorbed in the scenery, but by using their comments on it (its difference from or likeness to home) she can help them not to retire completely from pressure of present feeling. Children are not, of course, always sure that the feelings they have should be expressed; they may feel either that the adult will not allow it or that they themselves, for a variety of reasons, should not. Perhaps by telling a story of a similar situation, it may be possible to help the children appreciate that feelings are allowed. It may help children to deal with their feelings later if by her questions the worker draws out the memories and experiences of home they share together.

In this journey, then, the caseworker would be helping the children to see the problem, to express feelings about it, and to appreciate that there are positive factors in the situation, which mean that they are not lost and helpless.

(ii) *Beryl and Jennifer* (p. 41, *ante*)

This is a more complex situation, but the worker has perhaps more time to reach a solution. It can be used to illustrate a number of important points:—

(*a*) It is tempting, in view of Jennifer's problem, to overlook the problem of loyalty raised for Beryl by Jennifer's behaviour.

(*b*) The child care officer is in touch with both natural and foster parents, and it must be reassuring for the children if she can accept these relationships and remain steadily and reliably there, understanding the relationships but not taking sides. She will attempt to encourage both foster parents and natural parent to help Jennifer in this difficult situation, but this does seem to be a case in which, because of other features, supplementary help should be given to Jennifer in her own right.

(*c*) We should encourage Jennifer to think about the problem, and to discover its meaning for her. This will be accomplished by listening, by question and by suggestion (*e.g.* "when we are away from people we love we do not know what is happening to them, and we worry that they are not all right"). It is important that Jennifer is encouraged to work on the problem facing her at present (how to behave in the face of this conflict): the problem, in other words, is kept manageable. The caseworker may speculate about the Oedipal forces activating the present desire to return to father, but she will not share this with Jennifer. Such speculation may, however, help the worker to understand some of the forces at work, should Jennifer, for example, show a persistent desire to return to her father rather than take up the offer of a job she very much wanted some miles away.

(iii) *Gwen* (p. 41, *ante*)

In this case the worker is helping the child to form a new attachment to foster parents. In many situations of work with children in foster homes, child care officers often feel reluctant to work with the child for fear of spoiling or interfering with the relationship the child should be forming with the foster parents. One popular account of child care work in fact refers to the "ideal" situation in which foster parents are permitted to get on with the job without "interference" from the child care officer. This is a barren approach; non-intervention by itself achieves nothing. The value of the preparation of the child before he is placed in a foster home has been recognized in the Service, but what has not been fully assimilated is the necessity for direct work with the child in helping him prepare for, and engage in, new experience. Without help from the worker the child may take much longer, or even fail in the attempt, to assimilate the new experience of the foster home. This help, however, has a limited aim. In a fluid situation the caseworker because of compassion for the child's pain should not attract to herself the attachment of the child.

In the present case she might avoid this by helping the child see and accept a reasonable expectation of the home, and by connecting any feelings Gwen might express to the foster parents rather than to herself. The child is presenting a loyalty problem: Mother used to be angry when she played outside—what would Mother say about the foster home? I think that the worker should explore this a little, suggest perhaps that Gwen may wonder if her mother would be angry, and then that her mother does want the best for her and would be happy to know that she is settling in a new home. In view of the child's stage of development it would not be appropriate to discuss the child's probable feelings of responsibility for her mother's illness. At a later stage children may themselves bring this forward. (For example, Maureen (16) turns on the child care officer and says "It's all your fault. If you hadn't taken me away my mother wouldn't be in trouble".) What the worker would do for Gwen is to help her identify the particular aspect of her separation problem which she is presenting. She has progressed to the extent that she allows herself to experience further close relationships, but she is experiencing difficulty in dealing with feelings of disloyalty to her mother.

(iv) *Matthew* (9)

Matthew is truanting from school, having been returned home after a period in care. He is the eldest child in a "problem family", with a father apparently indifferent to children, and a mother who gives rough but adequate care as regards feeding and clothing, but seems incapable of controlling children once they cease to be babies. The family is being visited as a "preventitive" case.

This is a situation in which the natural parents are present. In this family it might be said that the objective would be to work with "the family as a whole". This does not, however, involve working with each family member, or with all the family problems It may be that offering Matthew help on his own will make the mother's other problems more bearable. In helping Matthew, the worker may well have to recognize with him feelings about separation from home and the officer's connection with it. This is an example of the different speeds at which administrative action and therapeutic help proceed. The officer as administrator is now concerned with prevention of future separation, as a person helping Matthew she may well have to work over with the child his feelings concerning the earlier action of the Department in separating him from his mother. The child care worker is, of course, more than a therapist; she is often in action, and is not only seen as powerful by children, parents and foster parents, but actually is so. It was indeed one of the purposes of the Children Act, 1948, that this should be so, and it is important that the administrative responsibilities and "therapeutic" activities of the child care worker should not be decisively split from one another. At the same time these activities are not mutually interchangeable. We should not carry over into the sphere of therapy attitudes and expectations more appropriate to administrative action. We judge administrative action by such criteria as speed in execution, but the child care officer as therapist will have to tolerate the very slow rate at which people's attitudes change.

In considering the possibility of helping Matthew directly it will be of interest to assess how much help the parents will allow him to receive. Will they perhaps see the offer exclusively as a criticism?

The importance of assessing the repercussions of direct help to children can be illustrated from the case of Pauline (14). Pauline was causing considerable distress by refusing to dispose of her sanitary towels properly and leaving them scattered over the house. The foster parents asked the worker to deal with the problem. The worker discussed the problem with Pauline in a non-critical manner, pointing out the inconvenience. She appealed to Pauline's wish to be grown-up and expressed her interest; she would like to know next time she called how Pauline was succeeding. She evidently communicated something, since the troublesome behaviour ceased. The foster mother, however, was resentful of the worker's success. This argues, it is suggested, not that the worker was wrong in dealing with the problem herself, but that she might have considered the repercussions of her action on the foster mother. It would be important in this case to take the earliest opportunity of recognizing some success of the foster mother and showing that the child care officer can "allow" success as well as understand failure.

(v) *Robert* (10)

Robert was in care as a result of a Fit Person Order made when he was six. He has previously been in care in a Children's Home for two years (3–5). His mother (48) was cohabiting with a married man and changed accommodation very frequently. The Children's Department decided to board Robert out.

2.5.56. Robert's mother writes to say she has found new permanent accommodation and wants Robert to be returned to her.

6.5.56. A home visit is made, and the child care officer forms the impression that both Robert's mother and the man she is living with (who is Robert's father) want Robert home. The Children's Officer writes to inform the mother that she could apply to the Juvenile Court for the revocation of the Fit Person Order.

10.5.56. The foster mother is informed that the mother sought a revocation. This is apparently accepted by the foster mother.

2.6.56. Robert's mother writes to the foster home, and the foster mother reports that Robert seemed to be very upset and asked not to be sent back to his mother. Mother visited.

12.7.56. Robert's mother applies to the Juvenile Court, but her application is turned down. This was due perhaps to the statement made by the Children's Department that Robert seemed to have settled well and that he had on more than one occasion said he did not want to return to his own mother.

The child care officer noted that during the proceedings Robert showed no interest in his mother. Once the Court had decided, however, that he could not at the moment return to her, he began to become restless, finally crying and shouting that he did want to return home to his own mother.

This extract illustrates that casework with children is not an episodic matter, but a means of continuing and developing understanding of the child and the problems he faces, so that he can face the crucial episodes of his life, with greater preparation. In view of Robert's unsettled past it is reasonable to suppose that the question of a return to his mother will cause considerable emotional problems for him. Some help might have been available from the foster parents. In view of the Children's Department's knowledge of, and intervention in, his past life, of the speed with which preparation had to be accomplished, and of the possibility of deep feeling preventing Robert talking this over with his foster parents, some help should have been given by the Department to this child. Robert, from his behaviour, is clearly facing the very difficult problem of feeling he has to choose between the foster home and his own mother. He must feel pulled in both directions, and it does not help if the Department allies itself, so to speak, with one side of his essentially two-sided feeling. The mother's visit to the foster home was a useful preliminary to beginning to help Robert to bring together these two parts of his life, but this should have been followed-up by more intervention on the part of the caseworker with the object, at least, of helping Robert to be prepared for how he might feel in court. The decision about a child's return home is always serious and usually also difficult. Part of the material for this decision will undoubtedly come from discussing the situation with the child, but it is not helpful for the child if he is not assisted to work out some of the two-way feelings he has about the situation. To accept at face value Robert's statement that he wanted to stay with his foster home is an unthinking attempt to respect the child's rights. He cannot decide such matters for himself or on his own.

(vi) *Muriel* (9)

Muriel has been admitted to a voluntary Children's Home. About four weeks after admission the child care officer calls to see her to discuss the future. The officer introduces herself, but Muriel remains silent. The officer says she has come to talk about Muriel's future. Muriel says that she wants to go home, that her mother said she could go home, that her younger brother, Billy, is at home.

Most of the other examples have shown the caseworker helping a child already involved in a natural or foster family. This extract illustrates the important part to be played by the caseworker in the lives of children in institutions. One of the unfortunate (if temporary) effects of the emphasis on boarding-out has been the neglect of children who, for one reason and another, spend most of their time in care in institutions. Some authorities now seek to ensure that each child, whatever kind of care is being promoted, has a child care officer concerned with and planning for his future. This kind of procedure emphasizes one of the most important problems in child care work, relationships between the residential and non-residential staff. This will be discussed later, but it is mentioned here as a background to any work with children in institutions. The same principle applies to this work as to all work with children, namely, as far as possible to help those who have daily care of a child to help that child more effectively, bearing in mind that a caseworker has specialist knowledge and special agency responsibilities.

In the case of Muriel, the child care officer is visiting because of a twofold responsibility to collect material as a basis both for planning future care and also for assessment of the extent to which effective care is being provided at the present. As the interview begins Muriel does not respond to the worker's introduction and it might have been useful to make some reference to the concrete tasks the worker has to perform as an explanation of her presence there. The announcement of "a discussion of the future" might have seemed a daunting task, but it elicits some response. Taking this lead from Muriel, the worker should "stay with" her in the present and help her to discuss the reasons for her coming into care and to express some of her feelings about them. This may well have been talked over between Muriel and the residential staff member responsible (indeed, it should have been), but it needs to be discussed again. Children have to try out feelings, explanations and answers many times and with different people before they become customary. Muriel will not proceed in this interview without some attempt to deal with these feelings, and their discussion is relevant to the issue to be resolved, what of the future.

In dealing with Muriel's statements about her present feelings it will clearly be insufficient for the worker to explain the present position in reality. She has the task of helping Muriel accept something of present reality, and she can perform this only by understanding what it is specifically about the present that hurts Muriel. In other words, a general explanation will fail, but an explanation

5

that has found and is addressed to specific anxieties stands a chance of success. Thus, the worker has to discover which of the three statements Muriel makes (about her own wretchedness at being away from home, her feeling of betrayal by her mother, her feeling of jealousy for her brother) she will respond to and discuss. Perhaps it would be useful to say something like "that sounds like a lot of unhappiness. Perhaps you wonder why you are here?" This may again elicit no response from Muriel, but a simple restatement of the reasons for admission often comes as a relief to children.

In this chapter some of the principles of casework with children have been applied to typical child care situations. On the whole the issue of casework service to the child, in contrast to a casework service on his behalf, has not been squarely faced in the child care field. It is suggested that thinking in terms of casework with children has a double benefit. First, our attention is drawn to ways of helping a child to discover and work on a specific problem. Thus, it is not sufficient to say this child is facing a problem of separation, but a particular problem in the separation experience, *e.g.* fear of new relationships. Secondly, we see again the indirect and direct part played by the relationship in the solution or alleviation of some of these problems. Casework with children may seem a very time-consuming activity in a Service already understaffed, but the child care officer has in the course of her statutory duty considerable contacts with children and performs many acts on their behalf. To think of a casework service is to reconsider the ways in which this contact and these acts might be more effectively used to help the child.

CHAPTER 4

CASEWORK WITH THE ADOLESCENT

"He will benefit from a framework that will limit his
sphere of activity to challenging but achievable and
acceptable goals."

JOSSELYN[1]

"He has one of those terribly weak natures that are not
susceptible to influence."

OSCAR WILDE[2]

THOSE who try to help adolescents are often confronted by behaviour
that is annoying, baffling or depressing. We frequently experience
similar emotions when we try through reading to improve the help
we offer. Well-rounded statements and high-sounding phrases
provide fleeting comfort from stubborn realities; we are soon left
feeling disenchantment if not disbelief. Why is the adolescent often
difficult to help? Can we do anything about it?

This chapter will be concerned with the help caseworkers might
offer to adolescents. There is no virtue in any attempt to describe
casework with any particular age range as a closed system, but by
considering the interaction of method and the chief characteristics
of any particular stage of personality development we may sharpen
our perception of both. No generalization can save us from taking
pains to understand the individuality of each case, but general
reflection may reveal principles that can be applied according to the
nature of the particular situation.

It is a significant if frustrating fact that the general condition of
knowledge about contemporary adolescents is characterized by a
surfeit of theory and a scarcity of practical investigation. We possess
a series of ideas that constitute some kind of model of the psychological development of the adolescent, but the absence of facts
prevents us from knowing how reliable the model is. Social workers,
however, should be accustomed to starting from and making the

[1] *The Adolescent and his World*, p. 76.   [2] *An Ideal Husband.*

best of a present position rather than dreaming of what they might accomplish if only they had more knowledge. Consequently, this chapter will begin with a brief summary of what we usually consider the main emotional problems of adolescence. An attempt will then be made to discuss the implications of this "knowledge" for case-work with adolescents. It is perhaps worth noting that writing on this subject is non-existent in England and extremely (and un-characteristically) meagre in the United States.

General Description

The adolescent can easily make us feel helpless. This is also likely to be the feeling of anyone faced with the problem of describing, briefly and generally, the condition of the adolescent. I shall rest content with a few simple observations useful to those attempting to help adolescents.

(1) The term covers a wide variety of behaviour and a consider-able age range.

(2) Granted this variety, there are common problems adolescents have to face sooner or later. These problems concern the personal, sexual and social identity of the individual adoles-cent. Once this identity has been established, the adolescent will have passed from infancy and childhood to adulthood.

(3) These problems are worked through at a time when parents may be particularly vulnerable.

(1) Although we refer to "adolescence" as if it was a familiar, clearly demarcated (readily observable) period of development, this is misleading. Adolescence is not a prescribed period of growth with definite characteristics observable in all "teenagers". It is the process of maturation, both physical and psychological, from child-hood through which every normal human being must pass. Every child becomes an adolescent at a particular phase in his own development. Some children are physical adolescents at a very early age, nine or ten perhaps, but may not become psychological adolescents until much later, thirteen or fourteen perhaps. With others the reverse is true. Some again may grow at a fairly equal rate psychologically and physically. There is, in other words, considerable variation between adolescents.

There is also considerable variation of behaviour within each adolescent. By this is meant not simply changes within any particular phase (*e.g.* change from spirituality to materialism or love to hate) but also changes between phases. We know very little about the phases of adolescence, but it is perhaps useful to consider adolescence as divided into three phases, early, middle and late. Limitation of space prevents a full characterization of these phases, and the following account will emphasize changes in social development.

In early adolescence we can see the beginnings of criticism of the physical features of the home. The adolescent is increasingly forgetful about household jobs previously undertaken quite willingly, and thoughtless about the needs of the family and the rights of individual family members. The early adolescent becomes less willing to accept parental direction and wants to be disassociated from younger brothers and sisters. He may find difficulty in managing school work, does not take a very active part in religious worship, and becomes unwilling to conform to the expectation of "authority" figures.

In middle adolescence the critical attitude towards the family turns towards family values. The adolescent may take more responsibility in the home, but this very often derives from a critical attitude towards the way parents fulfil these responsibilities. He competes with parents, and parental guidance is often replaced by that from outside "authorities". Outside the family the middle-adolescent assumes a more adult role, and begins to establish continuing relationships with his equals of either sex.

Late adolescence marks the beginning of full assumption of a mature role. There is in this phase a greater personal unity and an improved balance between satisfactions obtained inside and outside the home. There may be greater participation in religious practice and some acceptance of an adult position within the family. Adolescence may be said to terminate when physical and mental instability is replaced by psychological and bodily equilibrium; when the body structure develops and emotional crises are superseded by reasonably consistent ways of dealing with internal conflict.

(2) The adolescent attempts to discover what sort of person he is, and to establish an identity distinct from the image held by his family. In many ways he is faced with problems similar to those he has solved, more or less successfully, during his pre-school years. He

has to re-learn habits of personal cleanliness, to establish a sexual identity, and to deal with emotional ties within the family, particularly in regard to his mother and father. The problem presented by the triangular relationship of child–mother–father has to be faced again, but by an adolescent much more aware of himself as a sexual person. He also has to face a crisis of conscience. The character and content of the earlier conscience has, to some extent, to change. The rigid conscience of school years which, for example, forbade heterosexual love has to begin to allow such love and to learn to face and incorporate values other than the parental. Finally, the adolescent meets again some of the main anxieties of early life—anxieties concerning loss of love, failure to conform, and failure to love oneself. In brief, adolescence marks a recapitulation of many of the problems of infancy and early childhood, but these problems are faced by a more fully formed and stronger personality. In spite of this strength, however, the force of emotion at work often makes the ways of childhood and infancy seem very attractive. The adolescent often finds the prospect of independence overwhelming, and this may result in a return to dependence on the family, but this is soon seen as a threat to individual identity, and as renewing a dangerous connection between family and newly awakened sexual feeling.

(3) Generally, these problems are worked out within a family (or substitute family) and it is important to appreciate the stage of life reached by many parents when their children enter adolescence. Parents may be beginning to face the prospect of declining sexuality at a time when the sexuality of their children is bursting forth. They may have to face the fact that there are no longer prospects of advancement in a career. This realization comes just when the adolescent begins to dream and to plan for the future and to assert himself as an independent person. Both children and parents are also greatly influenced by the increasing pace of social change, which must emphasize differences between the generations. Where the possibility of so much contrast exists, conflict often ensues.

These general statements can perhaps do something more than reveal the extent of our ignorance. They may serve as a provisional description of adolescence from which we may form certain broad principles for casework action. These may be seen as (i) the families of adolescents are important; (ii) adolescence is a time of crisis of conscience; (iii) adolescents face the problem of identity; (iv) adolescents have difficulty in taking help. In order to illustrate the application of these principles and the difficulties presented to child care officers by many of their adolescents, the case history of one adolescent in care, Betty, will be presented. The four principles will then be discussed in the light of this and short extracts from other cases.

Betty (born 1.12.41)

An illegitimate child in the care of public authority from 31.12.41. In 1942 her mother was admitted to mental hospital and has remained there ever since.

1948

Betty is boarded out with Mr. Walker (51) and Mrs. Walker (48) and their adopted daughter, Geraldine (7). The Walkers want a companion for Geraldine and are willing to provide a home for another girl. This placement is reasonably successful, but trouble begins in 1955. In this year Mr. Walker has to go to mental hospital because of a depression. A home visit in November illustrates the effect this had on Betty and what the worker did:

8.11.55. Mr. Walker has been in the mental hospital and has returned home. Mrs. Walker complains that Betty is constantly answering her back. When Mr. Walker was in hospital she took advantage of the situation and was very difficult to manage. The worker pointed out that she had visited during that time, and Mrs. Walker had not complained. Mrs. Walker said she was too bothered and upset to tell her. During that time she was very distraught and lost a great deal of weight. She thinks that any upset with Betty will have a bad effect on Mr. W. The worker had a long talk with Betty and told her she must help as much as possible at the present time. Mrs. W. said she would ask for her removal, but this would be too upsetting for her husband. At the end of the interview the officer promised a further visit at the end of the month.

Difficulty with Betty continues until 17.6.57, when she is transferred to a small Family Group Home, following Mr. W.'s collapse. During this period the problem is seen partly as one of control on Betty's part and of consistency on the part of Mrs. W. The worker talked to Betty about the importance of self-control for her own sake and that of others. She also visited more frequently than statutorily required and gave Betty an occasional "talking to", as much to support Mrs. W. as to change Betty. These methods fail, however, and Betty is removed without preparation by the foster parents because she had become unmanageable when this had been previously discussed.

Betty does not settle in the Home and clings to the hope that she can return to the Walkers. They are very ambivalent about this, saying she can return if she shows an improvement in two weeks and then that there is no question of her coming back, only of her visiting them.

Later in the year they ask Betty to visit for a weekend, but the worker advises against this as she considers Betty is not yet emotionally independent of them. On 17.10.57 Betty is placed in a new foster home.

12.11.57. First visit since placement: Betty settled well. Had visited the Walkers. Worker said she thought it unwise for her to call very frequently, as the visits would provoke scenes and would unsettle her and prevent her settling with the Browns. Betty sulking and distant over this. Later Betty wondered if the worker could discover more about her parents and her brother. Worker said she could not see her brother because he was adopted. Betty imagined that she might meet him at a dance, fall in love and then discover the truth. Such things had happened, she said, and she had read of them in the papers. The worker told Betty that such an incident was extremely unlikely, and that as soon as she mentioned her name to the adoptive parents, they would realize. She said that one does not fall in love overnight. Betty listened to this with some acceptance, but was determined to know more of her parents and see her mother. She said she accepted that her mother was still in mental hospital. (The worker judged that she is not stable enough to see her mother in mental hospital, and that she cannot fully accept the fact of illegitimacy.) She arranged for Betty to go to the cinema as a birthday treat.

16.12.57. Mrs. Brown (the new foster mother) 'phoned the office. She had had a disagreement with Betty over money. Betty was spending a weekly amount well beyond her pocket money and would not say where the extra came from. Mrs. Brown is particularly sensitive about money and honesty where money is concerned. She feels she has to account to the Children's Department for all Betty's actions and expenditure. Worker said she would talk to Betty after the cinema visit.

17.12.57. Visit to cinema. Afterwards worker discusses Mrs. B.'s complaint with Betty. Betty felt that Mrs. B. did not trust her and she had, for this reason, been obstinate. The worker said that she would settle this matter with Mrs. B. on her behalf, but that in future she would have to settle financial matters with Mrs. B. herself; she would not be able to rely on the worker in the future to extricate her from similar situations. The worker emphasized that she would have to budget every week and accept Mrs. B.'s guidance willingly; Betty could not automatically expect Mr. and Mrs. Brown to believe her. She must be more forthcoming if she and Mrs. Brown were to understand one another. Betty promised to make an effort.

She reiterated her desire to see her brother. The worker told her this might be a lengthy and difficult business. She seemed to be less impatient about seeing her mother and she was convinced in her own mind that her mother is in a mental hospital.

19.12.57. Worker visited Mrs. Brown and told her Betty's explanation and asked her to accept it, whether she really believed it or not, as a basis of a new financial understanding with Betty. Mrs. Brown had discovered dishonesty in adolescents she had employed and this had made her very sensitive about honesty. She would not admit it, but she found it difficult to trust Betty. Apart from this she is considered a good foster mother. She had relations who were mentally ill, and can quote to Betty from personal experience.

8.1.58. Mrs. Brown 'phoned. Betty was making no effort to budget the spending money, and becoming more extravagant about things she wished to buy. Consistently overspending and could not account for money. Mrs. Brown tackled this directly, but Betty became obstinate and arrogant. She admitted finally she had been spending dinner money and taking food to work, unknown to Mrs. Brown. Recently after spending nearly all clothing allowance and Christmas gifts of money on a dance dress, Betty said she knew where she could get dance shoes for 8s. 6d. (the sum she had left). When at the shop, she said she would have a pair at 25s. 6d., thus forcing Mrs. Brown to buy them. Mrs. Brown felt Betty was exploiting her hospitality, and too big for her boots. Betty wanted to buy a bike at 8s. 6d. per week (total cost £23) and refused to consider a bike belonging to Mrs. Brown's daughter. She asked the worker to speak to Betty as she made no impression on her, and unless Betty was checked soon she felt she would use underhand methods to get money for all the things she wanted.

9.1.58. Worker visited and saw Betty, who admitted she had exploited Mrs Brown over the shoes and would not have done so if had not known Mrs. Brown could pay. She told worker how she spent her 9s. 6d. a week and it appeared she had little idea of spreading it. She was a complete optimist at the beginning of the week, and appeared genuinely muddled about money.

23.1.58. Letter from mental hospital (in response to enquiry from Children's Officer). Betty's mother still certified and a visit from daughter would not be wise.

14.3.58. Betty removed from Mrs. Brown because of illness of both foster parents. Betty in a temporary foster home.

16.5.58. Boarded out with Mr. and Mrs. Claw (both 58)—who had adopted a girl previously at the same convent as Betty. She had become very difficult but died a year ago in road accident. They were interested in Betty, whom they saw on visits to convent. Betty not very disturbed by move but resentful that the Browns' lodger stayed on. Rather apprehensive about future and wanted to return to town very quickly.

7.6.58. Visit of Betty to the Claws. Successful.

21.8.58. Betty had been difficult after holiday. She had refused all advice and been insolent. Now extravagant in demands and generally defiant. Worker explained that this is often a difficult period, with deprived children, following a very good beginning, and that Betty was not yet certain of their reactions to some forms of behaviour. Betty had said she had agreed to baby-sit at a friend's overnight and would go whenever they said. Claws had first said Betty should ask permission, and then that she could do what she liked. They said that they had decided that about many things she must learn by her own experience. They felt Betty was presupposing their refusal, and that too many scenes would engender more antagonism in her towards them.

Worker talked to Betty later and emphasized she was not satisfied that she was making enough effort to respect the C.'s wishes and fit in with the general routine of their household. Betty listened (as always) readily but soon forgot. She had told the C.'s she liked their home more than any other. (They have, however, very high moral standards and possibly Betty is reacting to their anxiety about her behaviour. Worker is not basically worried by this anxiety, because they are willing to accept guidance. Progress has been made.)

Betty asked again if she could see her mother. The C.'s said she intended to go as soon as she was 18. Worker said she could make new enquiries about her health. Betty always expressed a wish to see her mother when discontented or insecure.

15.9.58. Another letter to mental hospital asking that officer should visit and discuss Betty's mother's condition.

16.9.58. Reply from hospital. There would be no harm in visit of Betty, and certainly the child care officer could come. It was pointed out that the mother denied existence of Betty.

17.9.58. Home visit. Betty untidy and thoughtless, and no attempt to plan money. Scenes in which Betty insolent and then apologetic. C.'s tried to avoid such scenes unless over things they must make a stand on. Disturbed most by her habits of gossip on all subjects. Mrs. C. pleased with suggestion about Betty's visit to mother. She would support officer by talking to Betty first. Worker arranged to see Betty after seeing her mother.

25.9.58. Child care officer visited mother in hospital. She bore a strong physical resemblance to Betty. She talked pleasantly and rationally. Refused to admit she had a daughter, though the doctor the day before had persuaded her she had. She did talk of Betty's brother. She was confused and excited over personal matters and completely institutionalized.

30.9.58. Home visit. Saw the C.'s and Betty. Officer explained to Betty she had visited mother and intended to take Betty to see her. Betty very anxious to hear her impression of mother. She explained to Betty that mother would not admit having borne her; that Betty should not entertain any extravagant hopes of the visit and should be careful of subjects she talked of. She should on no occasion declare herself to her mother, as this would precipitate a scene. Worker discussed problem of mental illness at length. Betty was advised not to see this visit as leading to regular visiting. Future of her relationship with mother would depend on mother's reaction and success of the visit. It was possible mother would eventually accept her and would improve, but Betty should not be optimistic. Worker asked her to say as little as possible. Worker would ask about brother, her home, etc., so that Betty could satisfy her curiosity as much as possible. Betty accepted arguments in a reasonable manner, but whether she could absorb unpleasant facts emotionally was another matter.

13.10.58. Worker visited Mrs. Claw, who said she and Mr. Claw had talked to Betty about proposed visit to Hospital. Betty had generally been sensible, but she had said on one occasion mother would eventually recover and Betty could take care of her.

15.10.58. Visit with Betty to hospital. Betty calm and composed throughout. She did not speak much. Afterwards she commented on physical likeness between herself and mother. Also pleased mother had been strictly brought up and belonged to a respectable family. She asked if she could visit again and possibly regularly. Worker replied this was possible but must await doctor's opinion. Betty feared the C.'s might resent her visiting mother again.

4.12.58. Home visit. Considerable complaints. Betty insolent and independent. Quarrelled with boy friend and several girl friends. Mrs. C. felt Betty had no affection or consideration for them. Would not take advice; went into an hysterical rage and said they had no authority over her. (She was probably reactive to possessive and restrictive attitude of the C.'s).

4.12.58. Worker met Betty, warned her that unless she conformed to the C.'s standards she would have to leave. She accepted warnings sensibly. Bitter that they did not trust her, and felt they were talking to neighbours about her. Did not think their relatives liked her. Bitter about prospect of another move.

5.12.58. Worker visited clergyman—would he talk to the C.'s to prevent breakdown of placement? He said C.'s had serious doubts about Betty seeing her mother—they had told him. They did not want her to go ever again.

2.1.59. Letter from Claws asking for visit.

2.1.59. Home visit. C.'s had decided Betty must go. Mrs. C. said she had lost all affection for and interest in Betty because of her insolence and independent behaviour. Went dancing too often. Sometimes Betty would not talk to them and screamed wildly, rejecting their opinions instantly. She said they had no authority over her. Mrs. C. felt Betty looked on their home as lodging. She complained that their health had deteriorated. Worker asked Mrs. C. to reconsider. They had given Betty a final warning 3 weeks ago.

2.1.59. Worker visited clergyman and asked him to talk to Claws.

5.1.59. Home visit. Claws had not relented and had told Betty she must leave as soon as possible. Betty bitter and fatalistic—wanted a last chance. She reproached the Department for not finding a home that realized her hopes.

10.1.59. Betty saw the Children's Officer who reassured her that present placement had broken down because of incompatibility of temperament—if she was not happily settled by 18 the department would continue supervision as long as necessary.

22.1.59. Children's Officer saw Betty—no foster home yet. Betty pleased that she passed evening class exams. well.

29.1.59. Saw Betty. Officer told of possible home. Gave few details because she should judge for herself. She still wanted relationship with a family rather than lodgings.

2.2.59. Visited Mrs. Dent—willing to take Betty. Betty decided yes. Mrs. Dent (58) son of 15.

8.2.59. Betty boarded out.

19.2.59. Betty called at office. Settled well. Seemed to be considering words with more care, therefore learning by experience about her enthusiastic early feelings in other placements.
This placement went well and Mrs. Dent was helpful over Betty's visit to her mother.

5.6.59. Home Visit, to explain about visit to mother. Mrs. Dent said Betty had often talked of her mother. Betty was worried about girl of 15 at work expecting baby. Mrs. D. thought Betty was thinking of her mother. Betty very pleased when girl had had baby safely. Betty had told Mrs. D. that her mother's past was a lesson to her and she would not get herself into trouble. Mrs. D.'s tolerance and warmth had given her great stability. The foster parent form had not been signed until now, until Betty had settled and Mrs. Dent was prepared to keep her.

6.6.59. Visit to hospital. Betty brought mother a box of chocolates. Betty said the C.'s had said no one would wish to marry her if they knew her mother was in a mental hospital. Mother welcomed them warmly. Betty calm in the face of agitated elderly patients. Betty said afterwards that mother seemed more confused. Worker explained mother agitated by presence of other patients. She wanted to visit regularly—and worker arranged for Mrs. D. to visit with them next time, if possible. Betty was apprehensive about visiting alone once out of care. Afterwards Betty soon forgot her anxiety about her mother and talked willingly about general topics over tea.
Further boarding-out visits revealed good progress. Successful visit to mother with officer and Mrs. D.—Betty's brother was married and mother said of Betty—"Isn't she a pretty girl". Betty very pleased. Final visit saw Betty a success at work and well established in home enjoying domesticity.

April, 1960. Letter of thanks to staff and Children's Officer for kindness, understanding and help.

GENERAL PRINCIPLES OF CASEWORK HELP FOR ADOLESCENTS

The Families of Adolescents are Important

Because the adolescent seeks independence we often conclude that we can appropriately adopt towards him the sort of approach we usually make to adults. Clare Britton, for example, suggests that in the Child Care Service workers helping older children "will establish the caseworker–client relationship with which we are familiar, except that the worker's power and responsibility . . . will also be present . . .".[1] In some of our administrative regulations we assume a similar adult status. Thus, in the Memorandum on the Boarding-out Regulations (1955) it is stated that "since a child who is over

[1] Britton, C., *op. cit.*

compulsory school age is likely to be able to speak for himself, the minimum standard of visiting (of foster homes) is reduced ". This kind of approach to adolescents is sometimes accompanied by the assumption that parents of adolescents are expendable as far as casework help is concerned. Yet to stress the similarity between work with adolescents and with adults is to obscure the specific nature of early and middle adolescence, its precise character as neither childhood nor adulthood. As yet we know very little concerning the different kinds of help adolescents need as such, though it is possible that current research on their specific treatment requirements in psycho-analysis may throw some light on similar problems in casework.

It seems, however, that adolescents need their parents, and that if we try to help them we should take account of their need to work out some of their feelings in regard to their families, existent or non-existent. We should also see that we supply at this critical junction directly or indirectly the sort of help which families might provide.

Betty is obviously in need of a family, and is also consciously searching for one. She is in all placements but the last enthusiastically happy about each new home, but none is capable of withstanding her generally defiant, testing behaviour. To understand such behaviour is an important function of parents toward their adolescent children. In most families adolescents can rebel and yet, on the whole, remain fairly confident that the parents and the home will not disintegrate under the strain. For many boarded-out children, however, and children in residential accommodation this is an assumption that just cannot be trusted, as Betty has discovered. In fact Betty's experiences in care have heightened all the basic anxieties of adolescence—the anxiety that she has lost love, that she cannot conform, and that she herself could not love. If the adolescent begins to have serious difficulty in conforming to adult standards here she may begin to see adults entirely as a threat and may in addition fear that something is wrong with her. This fear is emphasized in Betty's case by the real facts about her mother, and by her fantasy that she is herself a dangerous person, having sent Mr. Walker (and, perhaps she feels, her mother) into a mental hospital.

Absence of a family means that the adolescent has little chance to work out the problem of dependence–independence. Betty clearly swings from angry attempts at independence to placatory promises of conformity. Yet in the changing circumstances of Betty's life the Children's Officer makes a creative use of an administrative provision when (10.1.59) she promises that the Department will not let Betty face the future alone if she has not settled in with a family when she is eighteen. The issue of dependence–independence is also an important feature of the various difficulties Betty encounters in connection with money. Problems in the use of money and the ways of leading an independent life are especially severe for adolescents whose whole previous existence has been in care.

In general, it may be said that failure to understand the part played by parents in the life of the adolescent may make it difficult for him to maintain a relationship with the worker. He may be led to dislike the worker because he feels the worker is encouraging him to grow up and become independent and such independence is too threatening. Adolescents may become much more dependent on their parents because of the fear of an independence now actively encouraged by another adult, the worker. An appreciation of the strength of these ties with the parent and of their ambivalent character may help us to approach the adolescent with more understanding.

Some adolescents are searching for their natural families, others need to be removed from them. The following case illustrates this latter necessity: Jennifer A. (16 years) is an after-care case from an approved school. The Children and Young Persons (Amendment) Act, 1952 gave local authorities specific power to arrange for after-care supervision at the request of approved school managers. This is difficult work, requiring close co-operation with school and home before the child leaves the institution. It is not surprising that this work often becomes the cinderella function of the Child Care Service. Jennifer is Mrs. A.'s illegitimate child. Three months after her birth, Mrs. A. was married but obtained a divorce in 1949. During the time the divorce was being made absolute, Jennifer was in a Children's Home for 12 months. In 1952 Mrs. A. married again and there is a child, Sheila, of the union.

> Jennifer is convinced she is rejected by her mother and there are constant clashes between them. Jennifer has no respect for authority or other people's property, and mother asserts she is sexually promiscuous (the doctor denies this). Mrs. A.'s present marriage is reasonably happy, but any rift within the home is attributed to Jennifer. Mrs. A. uses her husband as a threat and appears to fear

she will lose her husband and home. The officer noted a similarity of temperament between mother and daughter (*e.g.*, Mrs. A. is completely irresponsible regarding debts and appears highly strung). Mr. A. is more understanding of Jennifer, but his reaction to many of the family disturbances is to clear off to bed. Jennifer's attitude to Mr. A. is friendly, but she is afraid Mrs. A. is turning him against her.

A summary after the first 3 months of work states that peace was established at home when Jennifer was working away from home except for her day off. Mrs. A. appeared anxious when Jennifer was away from home.

This seems to be a case in which plans for Jennifer to work away from home, but maintain regular contact, should be considered. It appeared that Mrs. A. is projecting on to Jennifer some of the badness she feels in herself (*e.g.*, sexual promiscuity) and treating her as a potentially, if not actively, dangerous person who threatens her marriage. The relationship between mother and daughter contains strongly contradictory elements, and further exploration is necessary before the worker can be sure of the nature of the bond between them. Do they need this relationship, with all its seeming unsatisfying quality, so much that no physical separation can be maintained, or can they tolerate some easing of the tension? Only further work with the mother and child will show this, but if partial separation is decided on, *both* mother and daughter will require help. The mother will need help to feel this separation is part of a plan in which she, as the mother, has had a part otherwise her guilt may lead her to demand that Jennifer remains at home. Jennifer should be helped not to feel completely rejected. An important part of work with this family will be concerned with showing Jennifer that she has worth in the eyes of the worker, but casework cannot succeed for Jennifer unless Mrs. A. is also actively engaged.

The Crises of Conscience

One of the very few factual studies of adolescents in this country suggests that problems of forming and maintaining standards are important for the adolescent today. As the authors state: "there is great uncertainty about standards of behaviour, and much anxiety and confusion about roles and relationships in the home and at work."[1]

Briefly stated, the problems facing the adolescent can often be

[1] Logan and Goldberg, E. M., "Rising Eighteen in a London Suburb", *British Journal of Sociology*, Vol. 4, 1953.

usefully seen as problems about standards, about what *ought* to be done. The adolescent seeks standards to deal with the new situations (*e.g.*, Betty's problem with the handling of money when she begins work) and is faced with the abandonment or adjustment of old standards in the face of new. These old standards were supported by a fairly rigid child-conscience and the adolescent must now develop a more flexible conscience which allows some of the things formerly forbidden (*e.g.*, relationships with the opposite sex). Part of Betty's worry about the girl who is having an illegitimate baby is an anxiety that she herself might be capable of such behaviour. How might the caseworker help with this kind of problem? We are often given broad injunctions to meet such situations. We must "represent the standards of society", we are told. This is heartening, but only momentarily.

Consider the case of Jean (18) who was born in 1940, illegitimate, and who has been in care almost since birth. She is going to have an illegitimate baby. She goes to a Mother and Baby Home, and in a letter to her Children's Officer, she says she dreads what her friend Mabel will say. She writes to Mabel, who promptly spreads the news around. Jean writes again to the Children's Officer that she will eventually be returning to her home town, but feels everyone will look down on her. The Children's Officer replies:

> "Don't worry about the girls knowing ... Everyone knows you are not in any way an immoral girl, and whereas people might blame you and have no sympathy for you if you had been behaving foolishly, I feel quite sure they will understand that someone has taken advantage of your lack of experience, and will not in any sense look down on you. There is no shame whatsoever attached to having a baby if you, yourself, have not been guilty of intentionally wrong behaviour, and I think you must regard this like I do. It is unfortunate, but it can be lived through without upsetting your future in any way provided you are sensible about it ..."

It must first be noted that this is an attempt to deal with a problem by letter and not direct contact. This increases the difficulty for the Children's Officer, but in cases of this kind much important work has to be accomplished by these means. The general tone of this letter is perhaps over-optimistic and falsely reassuring, but it is in other ways helpful. It discusses Jean's anxiety about people's possible reaction to her condition and also clearly indicates not only that the worker does not blame her, but that the future can be assured, provided Jean plays her part. This statement of hope, and the accompanying expectation that Jean has a part to play, is both realistic and helpful. What is difficult to accomplish by letter, but remains a necessary task, is to elucidate Jean's reaction to the suggestion that as a victim of inexperience she is not to blame. The letter deals with the problem as it is presented, *i.e.*, as a reality problem (how can she in fact manage the difficult task of a return home in view of other people's feelings). Yet, we must wonder if Jean feels responsible for the pregnancy, no matter what its circumstance. How far is Jean concerned not simply with the opinion of others, but also with her opinion of herself (*i.e.*, with the problem as one of conscience)?

In other situations, the worker is concerned not with feelings about actions in the past, but with helping the adolescent to manage day-to-day problems which involve standards of behaviour. For example, the worker in the case of Peter (16), who has been convicted of maliciously wounding his older brother, advises him that he should maintain a neutral attitude towards his brother in the home. In the case of Gloria (16), the child care officer, dealing with an adolescent who cannot manage her income, advises her on the keeping of a budget and tells her to open a Post-Office account; the officer says she will look at the Post Office book from time to time. In these two cases the workers are outlining a standard of behaviour. This is what the Claws failed to do in the case of Betty (see interview 21.8.58). It is important not only that such an outline is clear, simple and steadily maintained, but also that it is offered in a way that makes it not too difficult for the adolescent to accept. In Peter's case, the officer, whilst clearly indicating that certain behaviour will be considered wrong, should show equally clearly that limits are not put on feelings. Peter should feel free to talk about and express his feelings within his interviews with the officer. With Gloria and with Betty, it is important to appreciate what meaning money may have in view of the history of deprivation. The officer may, for example, find it useful to say in words and attitude: "You feel you've had to go without when you were young. Now you are earning for yourself you want to buy lots of things. But you can hold on to some of what you've earned, and I want to help you do this." Obviously this takes many interviews to say, but it does summarize the feelings the adolescents may be expressing in different degrees—the need to

6

assert independence by spending as they wish, and the feeling that they cannot hold on to any good (money and the valuation of their work money represents).

The Problem of Identity

As we have seen, the adolescent is seeking a sexual, personal and social identity. This is rarely achieved with ease and many adolescents in care have had experiences similar to those of Betty. Their puzzlement about the kind of person they are must sometimes be emphasized by social and administrative rearrangements that occur about this time. The adolescent may have to move not simply from school to work, but also from a female to a male child care officer, from a children's home to hostel or lodging, and from home to a probation hostel or approved school. This kind of change makes it very important for the worker to maintain for the adolescent a firm image of himself as a person. This is all the more important when, as frequently happens, casework has to be supplemented by, or follows after, a period of residential care.

In order to foster the growing sense of identity, the caseworker emphasizes positive factors in the adolescent, and helps him to develop satisfactory identifications. A sense of personal identity is based on acknowledgement of sameness with, and difference from, the parent of the same sex. The worker emphasizes not simply possible achievement and intention, but also the integrating force that is at work. By this I mean that in his comments the worker will not lay stress on rapidly changing feeling (Today you feel this: yesterday you felt that etc.) but try to elucidate the central themes of effort and intention.

> Take, for example, the case of Michael (16), in care since the age of 5. His parents were prosecuted for neglect. He has had no stable placement in care, having had a series of foster homes and periods in residential homes. After he began work he expressed a wish to contact his parents. He was encouraged in this by the child care officer. He receives the following letter from his mother:
>
> "Michael,
> You can forget about coming here ... It is silly to say you miss us; you never knew us. Don't bother me again. The answer will always be no.
> Your Mother."

In this case we see again that casework with children must recognize the part played by parents even when they are physically absent and have been so for a long time. Physical separation does not mean emotional disengagement. Michael, at this particular period in his life, is concerned with the problem of identity—what kind of person is he? He is encouraged to contact his parents because one of the ways of finding out what he is like is for him to come to terms with what his parents are like. His initiative is rebuffed, and if future initiative is met in the same way, Michael may easily become a withdrawn, discouraged person with little sense of his own worth. This tells us something about the way the caseworker should attempt to help him. His problem is severe, but adolescence is a time of change and hope, and it has been argued that even the effects of early deprivation can be undone if appropriate treatment is available. This, however, is not the task of the caseworker. The caseworker might take, as the problem to be dealt with, Michael's work difficulties. These must be seen in the context of more basic problems, but the way the caseworker helps Michael with his job will also help Michael with his problems of initiative, identity, etc. The worker should encourage him to talk about the job, its difficulties and interests and possible alternatives. Michael's suggestions must be valued, though they may not be realistic enough for action. For example, when, after a period in hospital, Michael tells the worker that he did not appreciate that there were other people less well-off than himself and that he would like to be a male nurse, the worker valued the desire for reparation behind the wish, even though the project was unrealistic. This last comment illustrates the importance of casework being undertaken by the Department which, in Clare Britton's words, holds "continuity" for the child. It was necessary for Michael to make his offer of reparation to someone who was in the place of his parents, who had some meaning for him and who could, as it were in place of his parents, accept restitution for the hatred originally directed against them.

Betty, in showing concern about her brother and mother, is also seeking a solution to her problem of identity. Here the Department helps her with persistence in requesting the co-operation of the mental hospital and with careful arrangements for the actual visiting of Betty's mother. This has clearly been an important therapeutic experience for Betty, especially in view of her statement (whether true or not) that the Claws had said no one would marry her once they knew her mother was in a mental hospital.

Problems in Taking Help

Adolescents appreciate and need new experiences and it would be incorrect to assume that all adults are suspect in their eyes. This is a period (particularly in mid-adolescence) when there is a search for a hero and it is to be hoped that many of the adults who try to help adolescents become for them hero figures. Yet it is important to recognize some of the difficulties involved for adolescents in taking help. They may have expected punishment or may fear they will be "understood" or that their demands will not, cannot, be met. The adolescent may become dependent on the worker and this may be alarming for both. Yet dependency as such is neither good nor bad; what matters is the circumstance of the dependency and what is being sought in the dependency.

It is not true that help is automatically suspected by the adolescent simply because it comes from an adult. Betty has derived help from her contact with child care workers as have several others described in this chapter. What has helped them has been the extent to which the worker could understand and express some understanding of their specific worries and anxieties, without their having to be too explicit themselves in describing them. In other words, we do not talk to adolescents too insistently about our desire to "help", but we try to show that we can be trusted and actually are of some use to them. We cannot expect them to be very articulate about their problems; we should expect that we can view their difficult behaviour very often as an expression of an underlying anxiety.

This does not mean that we allow adolescents to bask in uncritical acceptance of all they do. Attempts are made in the case of Betty, for example, to control her behaviour, though perhaps enough attention is not always given to her feelings about both the attempts at control and the behaviour in question. An extract from the case of Patricia illustrates control helpfully exercised, at the same time as some recognition of her feeling is given.

Patricia (born 1940), was committed to care as beyond control and in need of care or protection in 1951. In 1955 she is placed in a Training Home run as a boarding school. In August, 1956, she writes to the child care officer:

> "I am very truly sorry to tell you I cannot live here another week. I must come back, it's driving me really and truly mad. I feel I can

speak to you because you have understood me more than most people. That's why I am pleading with you . . . I must leave at once. I *plead* with you."

The Children's Officer replies as follows:—

"Your letter this morning gave me quite a shock, and I cannot imagine what has caused you to write in such a strain. You are bound to feel very home-sick for two or three weeks [after the holiday], and I am wondering if this natural feeling could account for your present mood.

We are, as you know, very busy and the officers are working very long hours so it is not easy to release anyone to travel to X to talk over what is in your mind, but if you can be patient I will try to make arrangements for Miss B. to come to see you next week if you *still feel that life is unbearable at the end of this time*, and on the understanding that you make some effort to settle down.

There is no doubt that to give a term's notice is the correct course. This would be fair to the Headmistress and would give me some time to arrange somewhere suitable for you to live. There is no vacancy at . . . Also, as you realize, sleeping accommodation is not satisfactory at . . .

I am glad you enjoyed the holiday and I hope you will keep good faith by not doing anything stupid on an impulse. It may impose some strain on you for a few days, but I really feel pretty confident that you have reached the stage where one can talk to you in an adult way, and that you will react as an adult and not as a child any longer. Will you please write by Friday to let me know if it is quite essential for Miss B. to come down next week.

Again a difficult task is being attempted by letter, but the attempt is made to express some sympathy with Patricia's strong feeling and also to present the reality of busy conditions of work, notice, etc. At the same time the Children's Officer tries to show confidence that Patrica is an adult and will try to act as a grown-up. It is difficult to see if this latter attempt will prove effective, but it is sometimes helpful to adopt a role which is the opposite of that demanded of the worker by the adolescent. For example, to help an adolescent to be grown-up when he is expressing dependency, or to offer responsibility when he feels irresponsible. We have, however, always to be sure that such a challenge will not prove overwhelming.

Finally, there is a danger that we will, in attempting to help adolescents with their problems, see only the problems and not the opportunities this period of growth affords. We should not ourselves become too anxious about the problems or our capacity to help. Some writers see working with adolescents as a most complex and delicate operation. "Youth work", says the Albemarle Report, "is peculiarly challenging precisely because it requires a tense day-to-day walking on a razor-edge between sympathy and surrender".[1] Niceness of phrase cannot conceal anxieties behind this image of the worker's performance, which, unless faced and reduced, could make work with adolescents hesitantly coy or constrictedly distant.

[1] *Youth Service in England and Wales* (Albermarle Report), November, 1958, p. 40.

CHAPTER 5

FOSTER PARENTS AND THE CHILD CARE OFFICER (1)

BOARDING-OUT as a means of helping children deprived of a normal home life has a long history. In Glasgow, for example, which has at present a very high rate of boarding-out, this method of care has been used for over 170 years.[1] Heywood[2] has published a full account of a case of boarding-out in 1808 in which the Wordsworths were interested. Yet in spite of legislation concerning the selection and supervision of foster homes (from 1782, at least) and the growing official recognition of foster care in the second half of the nineteenth century, the essential features of such care as we know it today are of very recent origin. Before the Children Act of 1948 administration of foster care was far from uniform in practice, and uncertain from the point of view of either efficiency or benevolence. It is only in the last two decades that we have begun to apply our growing knowledge of human relations and personality development to the formulation and understanding of the functions and motive forces of fostering.

The present-day emphasis on foster care can be seen from the way in which the Children Act, 1948 treats "the mode of provision of accommodation and maintenance" in section 12(1):

"(1) Subject to the provisions of this section a local authority shall discharge their duty to provide accommodation and maintenance for a child in their care—

(a) by boarding him out . . . or

(b) *where it is not practicable or desirable for the time being* [my italics] to make arrangements for boarding-out, by maintaining the child in a home . . . or by placing him in a voluntary home . . ."

The place given to boarding-out in the new Child Care Service

---

[1] For some illustrations of this work see Brough, R., "One Hundred Years of Boarding-Out", *Child Care*, January, 1954.

[2] Heywood, J., "Boarding-out and the Wordsworth's", *Case Conference*, November, 1959.

was further enhanced by pressures to economize. Indeed, the Select Committee on Estimates (1951/2) were so impressed by the economic advantages of foster care that they conceived of the institution as a place of "recuperation" before boarding-out, or even as a place of "training" so that children might become "suitable for boarding-out, if they are not suitable when first coming into care".[1] The Report of this Committee was undoubedly one of the pressures which made Children's Officers continue to look anxiously at the percentage of children boarded-out, since it seemed that this was to be taken as the main index by which their work would be judged. In this respect the finding of the recent survey that there was a tendency for a higher proportion of placements to break down in areas with a high boarding-out rate than in areas with a low rate is worth some attention.[2]

The popularity of foster care comes at a time when a new child care policy is changing the character of traditional fostering. The Children's Officer for Birmingham commented that

"practically every offer of a foster home received by the department in the last four years has been an offer to take a child who has no parents or relatives to whom he is likely to return and who can, therefore, be boarded-out permanently. In other words, practically every offer has been a near-adoption offer."[3]

For many children this will constitute a helpful measure, but many others will be in the care of the local authority for a short period only.

"About half the children coming into care in the course of a year are received because of temporary difficulties in the home, usually confinement or temporary illness of the mother, and many children remain in care for only a few weeks."[4]

This means that short-stay fostering has become an important feature of the child care service.

[1] Sixth Report from the Select Committee on Estimates, 1951-2, p. xxi.
[2] Gray, P. G., and Parr, E. A., "Children in Care and the Recruitment of Foster-Parents", *Social Survey*, 1957, p. 31.
It is suggested that authorities with higher boarding-out rates may be more optimistic than others about the permanence of the homes chosen. At the same time the survey notes (p. 32) that "areas with a high boarding-out rate succeed in boarding out a correspondingly high proportion of the children who are generally thought to be more difficult, namely those in care under Fit Person Orders ... whereas areas with a low overall boarding-out rate have an even lower rate among such children".
[3] *The First Four Years* (cited at p. 22, *ante*).
[4] Seventh Report on the Work of the Children's Department, 1955, p. 1.

Another change in policy which affects foster care is the emphasis given in the 1948 Act to the child's original home and family.

In the case of children received under section 1 the local authority has a duty

"in all cases where it appears to them consistent with the welfare of the child so to do, [to] endeavour to secure that the care of the child is taken over either—
(a) by a parent or guardian of his, or
(b) by a relative or friend of his . . ."

Parents have a duty to maintain contact with local authorities. Since the 1948 Act local authorities have been giving increasing attention to the rehabilitation of the child in his own family, and to what is loosely termed "preventive work" in the child's own home. Present child care policy places the child very much in the context of his family. This means that foster parents enter not only into relationships with a child, but also, in varying degrees, with his natural parents. It also marks a reversal of the "fresh start" theory of boarding-out which was current in the late nineteenth and early twentieth centuries. As a writer in 1904 stated, "There can be no doubt that fresh country, fresh surroundings, and a fresh home mean in most cases a fresh start, and *that* after all is what we want to give our children".[1]

The present position is that foster care has been given great importance, but that its character is changing. Changes in policy and in knowledge affect "traditional" fostering, and also make the task of the child care officer in relation to foster parents one of considerable intricacy.

The view that the role of the worker in foster placement is essentially complex is thus of recent origin, but fragmentary recognition has been given in the past to some of its complicating undertones. When fostering was first extensively and officially used in England towards the end of the last century, the official visitor was seen primarily as an inspector, whose chief way of working was through the surprise visit and the meticulous examination of the child. "It is quite possible to visit and see children continually and yet know nothing of their true condition" reported Miss Mason in 1893, "if no real examination is made underneath."[2] Yet Miss

[1] Birchall, J. D., "Boarded-out", a paper read to the 25th Annual Poor Law Conference for the West Midland District, 1904.
[2] 22 Local Government Board, 1892/3, p. 119.

Mason saw this kind of examination as an act of fairness towards the foster parents as well as a scrutiny of their care. She stated that, "If I find a child clean, I always report the fact to the foster parent's credit".[1] Some of the evidence to the Mundella Committee on Poor Law Schools in 1896, whilst emphasizing the importance of inspection, also mentioned the value of upholding the foster parents' sense of responsibility for the care of the child.

The largely inspectoral role of the visitor was slowly abandoned, but no clearly formulated alternative to the firm position outlined in Miss Mason's reports was found. To some writers the visitor was a friend, chatting and (inevitably) drinking tea; to others something between a friend and an inspector. Some American writers saw the caseworker as giving "practical training" to foster parents,[2] but this viewpoint does not appear to have been canvassed in England. The Report of the Curtis Committee (1946) emphasized the value of boarding-out, but in spite of its attention to the training of fieldwork staff it gave no detailed view of the content of their work in this connection. The boarding-out officer required "skill in handling personal relations" (Appendix I) and some salaried officials were commended for the "easy and happy relationship between the visitor and the whole family" (p. 122). Emphasis since the beginning of the new unified Child Care Service seems to have been on skill in the selection of foster parents, rather than on exploration of the way in which these parents, once chosen, could be helped to overcome difficulties, and to achieve greater satisfaction as foster parents. With few exceptions, writing on the Child Care Service since the Curtis Report has done little to extend our skill in, or expand our understanding of, work with foster parents. American literature on the subject is considerable[3] in extent and often exciting in tone, but differences of agency setting and an extravagant and sometimes precious view of the work have not made it an easy source for child care workers to approach.

The essence of the child care officer's work with foster parents is to choose them and help them to take into their home and care for

---

[1] 21 London Government Board, 1891/2, p. 195.

[2] *E.g.* "Home-finding is, then, the process of selection of volunteers, and home supervision is a continuous process of practical training", Doran, M., and Reynolds, B., *The Selection of Fosterhomes for Children*, 1919.

[3] Not simply the contemporary literature. As early as April, 1931, Towle contributed to the *American Journal of Orthopsychiatry* "The Evaluation and Management of the Marital Situation in Foster Homes".

the child or children of other parents. This work is neither simple nor easy, and part of its complexity is due to a failure to grasp the characteristics of the kind of relationship appropriate to the task. The relationship between foster parent and child care officer has some resemblance to other relationships with which each is already familiar. Foster parents, in some respects, are applying to do a job of work. They may become working partners with the child care officer, who may also find some of her casework skills useful in her contacts with them. The relationships may seem to resemble that between client and caseworker[1] or caseworker and supervisor.[2] Yet such statements, though they may partially illuminate the relationship, offer no exhaustive description. Each describes a necessary aspect of work with foster parents; none represents a sufficient characterization of the whole.

The aim of this chapter is to examine aspects of present work with foster parents, beginning with the task of selection. An attempt will be made in the following chapter to characterize the problems that commonly arise in foster care and to suggest generally how these might be handled.

Choosing Foster Parents

The social worker who attempts to choose foster parents is faced with difficulties of role, of knowledge and of skill. Something will be said of each of these in turn.

In selecting applicants the social worker finds herself in the unaccustomed position of judging people in regard to their suitability for her purposes, and *of rejecting* those who are unsuitable. In accepting and rejecting offers of service, the social worker has a responsibility both to the child and to the applicant. The applicant must be chosen in a way that provides a good basis for future work or rejected in a way that lessens a sense of worthlessness. This latter is important, not simply because of its implicit recognition of social work values, but also because of its possible effect on local valuation of the Department's work. During the phase of investigation of the foster home the worker may feel some uncertainty, in view of the

[1] See, *e.g.*, "Modern practice in home-finding . . . is no longer generally subordinate to or isolated from the steady growth of casework, but it is casework" Hutchinson, D., *In Quest of Foster Parents*, 1943, p. 6.
[2] This analogy is frequently drawn in the American literature. See, for example, Glickman, E., *Child Placement through Clinically Oriented Casework*, 1957, p. 199.

fact that the applicant comes to offer a service rather than to seek help with a problem. In brief, the role of selecting foster homes may be more or less unaccustomed for the social worker, containing possibilities for doubt and, if the application is rejected, guilt.

General Knowledge

We have seen that caseworkers attempt to use knowledge to understand a problem, and that they acquire particular knowledge about each individual case (investigation or diagnosis). What does the child care officer know that can help her in selecting foster parents? What areas of feeeling and behaviour in foster parents and children does she need to explore before reaching a decision that "the household of the foster parents is likely to suit the *particular* needs of the child"[1] [my italics]? It is obvious that no generalization can make the decision on the officer's behalf. No amount of research on past breakdowns in foster homes can secure automatic success with any particular selection. Yet such knowledge as we have can supply some guide lines for action. What is this knowledge?

It can be divided into three main kinds, knowledge of stages of personality development, an approach connected with the theory of maternal deprivation and knowledge derived from the study of fostering practice in the child care service. The stages of development have been discussed, and some aspects of theories of maternal separation and deprivation have already been considered in Chapter 2. These theories, connected with the name of Bowlby in this country, have undoubtedly contributed to the popularity of fostering, but in this chapter their implications for the selection of foster parents are considered briefly. These implications relate to the problems facing the child separated from his home; we need some idea of these problems so that we can look for people likely to help in their solution.

Wootton has devoted a chapter in her *Social Science and Social Pathology* to Theories of the Effects of Maternal Separation or Deprivation. She concludes by considering the view that such theories may be taken as "suggestive".

> "But," she asks, "suggestive of what? Of the fact that a child needs a warm continuous relationship with a mother or mother-substitute or,

[1] Boarding-Out of Children Regulations, 1955, reg. 17.

in still simpler terms, of the fact that children (like their elders) need to be dependably loved, and that without such dependable love, they are likely to become frightened, unhappy or mentally retarded? It is indeed a melancholy conclusion that it should have been thought necessary to employ so much costly research with so pretentious a scientific façade, in order to demonstrate these homely truths".[1]

This brisk summary obscures more than it clarifies. It neglects the variety of unhappiness, ranging from emotional upset to very serious withdrawal. Lewis has described what may be seen as the minimum of unhappiness:

"The majority of the children were unsure of themselves, eager for adult approval, easily discouraged, and anxious to be with their parents . . . The most striking and painful feature of most of them was their emotional upset."[2]

At the other end of the scale we find children withdrawn from the environment, mistrustful of others and themselves, caught up in their own inner world. Children filmed in "Maternal Deprivation"[3] are compelling and distressing examples of this. This variety of outcome, stressed in Bowlby's later research,[4] underlines the importance of individual study in each case so that the particular effects of separation can be revealed.

In separating the child from his parents, we present the child with specific and serious psychological problems. He has, firstly, to manage feelings aroused by the event. The child feels he has deserted or been deserted by, his parents, that he has lost something of himself. Who is to blame? Who is to blame that he feels lost, that he feels he has lost some good that he had? He may blame and hate his parents or himself, and such feelings may be behind Goldfarb's association of aggressive and overactive behaviour with institutional experience in infancy.[5] Burlingham and Freud have given an example of a child who feels intense hatred for a previously loved person who left him.[6]

These are the feelings aroused by separation from the mother or

[1] Wootton, B., *op. cit.*, p. 154.

[2] Lewis, H., *op. cit.*, p. 122.

[3] Aubry, J., and Appell, G., *Maternal Deprivation in Young Children* (obtainable from Tavistock Child Development Research Unit, 2 Beaumont St., London, W.1).

[4] Bowlby, J., Ainsworth, M., and Rosenbluth, D., "The Effects of mother-child separation: A follow-up study", *British Journal of Medical Psychology*, Vol. 29, 1956

[5] Goldfarb, W., "Infant Rearing and Problem Behaviour", *American Journal of Orthopsychiatry*, Vol. 13, pp. 249–265, 1943.

[6] Burlingham, D., and Freud, A., *Infants without Families*, 1947.

mother substitute for any length of time. Other feelings can be expected to develop when the child has to face new parent figures and to deal with the threat of his incipient feelings of love towards them and of the possibility of another separation from them. To deal with these feelings, the child will handle the situation in a number of different ways. He may seek to repeat the past, so that his anger towards his foster parents appears justified. He may split his feelings, so that the foster mother is seen as all bad. He will probably use one or two main methods for dealing with problems in feeling, and if these can be identified in the child's history, some useful indications can be obtained for the selection of foster parents who will not be too vulnerable to the particular methods used by the child.

Studies of the practice of foster care provide several useful guides for the choice of foster parents. They all emphasize the importance of the child's previous experience. Baxter, for example, in a small case study, suggested that children tended to develop foster family relationships based on attitudes similar to those displayed at home.[1] Trasler's more extensive and sustained study of 57 foster home failures contrasted with a group of 81 successes, emphasizes

> "the effects upon the child of previous experiences of rejection by the parents or by foster parents. The disturbances set up by these events appear to have contributed to more than half of all the foster home breakdowns studied."[2] "More than three-quarters of those children admitted to public care before the age of five years who subsequently failed in their foster homes spent at least half of the first years of life in institutions; only 40% of those whose foster home placements were successful experienced as much institutional care as this in infancy."[3]

A smaller study by the same author draws attention to the relationship between early experience of institutional care and failure in a foster home placement.[4] Other work indicates the important part played by the attitudes of children to their natural parents. Conflicting feelings towards them can be carried over easily to the foster parents.[5] These researches thus emphasize the importance of

---

[1] Baxter, A., "The Adjustment of Children to Foster-Homes, Six Case Studies", *Smith College Studies in Social Work*, Vol. VIII, No. 3, March, 1937.

[2] Trasler, G., *op. cit.*, p. 203.

[3] *Ibid.*, p. 211.

[4] Trasler, G., "The Effect of Institutional Care upon Emotional Development", *Case Conference*, June, 1957.

[5] Gardner, G. E., "Ambivalence as a Factor in Home Placement Failure", *American Journal of Orthopsychiatry*, Vol. XII, No. 1, January, 1942.

securing as full a history as possible of the pre-placement experience of each child. The history will indicate length of separation and periods at which it occurred, the previous ways that the child has handled this and other kinds of stress, and his predominant attitudes to his natural parents.

Other factors that studies indicate as important are the expectations and fears of foster mothers. Trasler, for example, discusses a number of cases of foster homes which failed because the child was unable to fill the roles which the foster parents had planned for him.[1] There has been very little study made of foster parents, but a survey of boarding-out placements in 1956 gave some useful general information.[2] The sample of foster mothers was asked what prevented people from fostering: 37% thought it was fear of how the child would develop and of his background, and 19% gave as an answer, fear of losing a child once you have grown fond of him. It is possible that these answers indicate some of their present fears about their own foster children. Bowlby[3] has quoted Mulock Howrer's finding that the placement of a foster child of the same age and sex as the child of foster parents caused friction. Trasler also found that the age of the child at placement and the age of the foster mother were of some significance. Two-thirds of those placed before the age of 4 were judged to have achieved a good foster home adjustment, but of those placed between 7 and 13 about 70% were later removed from foster homes. A large proportion of failures in all homes were found in foster mothers under 40. The 1956 survey indicates that 27% of our foster mothers are in this age range.

Such knowledge as we have—partly experience based on consideration of theories of separation, partly extensive and intensive studies—is extremely limited. It can be best used to indicate risk and to suggest that particular areas should be studied in foster parent applications. It should not be used to support any kind of absolute notion of "the good" foster home and "the bad" nor to encourage assessment in terms of single factors, negative or positive. Bowlby's list of findings from the work of Howrer and Isaacs does in fact suggest a single factor approach, particularly when he talks of these findings in terms of "situations to be avoided wherever possible". Situations to be avoided include the placement of young

[1] Trasler, G., *op. cit.*, Chapter 5.
[2] Gray, P. G., and Parr, E. A., *op. cit.*, p. 39.
[3] Bowlby, J., *Maternal Care and Mental Health*, 1952.

children with foster parents over 45, whilst positive situations include the presence of the foster parents' own children. Yet what sort of "guidance for practice" is this when we know from the 1956 survey that 43% of foster children are placed with foster mothers of 41 and over and that 36% of foster mothers were childless? Does this mean that a high proportion of foster homes were not successful or that there were other factors in the situation which balanced the risks? The latter seems more likely. A particular combination of attitudes and circumstances seems to lead to success in one case and failure in another. Yet decisions have to be reached, and it is clear that in our enthusiasm for fostering these decisions are not always wisely made. The 1956 survey suggested that at least 17% of foster home breakdowns were probably the result of an unwise choice of foster parents.

Knowledge of the Individual Applicant

Faced with this responsible decision, and armed with some knowledge, what does the child care officer need to know of the foster home before she can accept or reject a particular application? When confronted with the complex task of judging and selecting foster parents, it is natural either to seek some relatively simple criterion or to assume that we should approximate to an ideal position in which as much information as possible is collected. Some idea of the sort of information required by those who seem to adopt the second approach can be gained from the following rather breathless list:

> "During her visits to prospective foster parents, the Children's Officer seeks to form an impression of the home and family as it is; the standard of living achieved and aspired to; the education and background of the parents, and its effect on their views regarding the upbringing of their own children and foster children; the level of development and behaviour of the applicant's own children; the standard of housekeeping; the different temperaments and outlook of husband and wife; and their ability to tolerate difficulties (such as bed-wetting) which may arise if a child is placed. She tries to assess the cohesion and emotional atmosphere of the family group, and to foresee the result of the impact of a foster child, and from her ideas emerges the picture of the sort of child who may be expected to succeed, with, of course, special reference to any special interests or hobbies of the family."[1]

[1] *The First Four Years*, p. 82, *op. cit.*, p. 22, *ante.*

There is a danger perhaps with this sort of approach, which examines the possible future as well as the actual present, that a large number of items are collected which do not, taken together, form a clear picture of the prospective foster parents as people. There is, moreover, quite a severe restriction on the amount of information anyone can use in coming to a decision.[1] It is preferable to concentrate on the actual process of application in the "here and now", and to develop the study of the applicants through three or four key themes. This will be considered below.

The other approach (the attempt to use a relatively simple criterion) sometimes appears in the statement that the "neurotic" applicant should be discovered and rejected. If this term is used with any care, the argument assumes a fairly high degree of diagnostic ability. It also implicitly supports a single factor approach, whereas the argument of this chapter is that we need to look not at single factors, but at the interrelationship of factors. Another argument that uses a simple criterion is that which emphasizes the motives of foster parents. The term "motives" is used very loosely in social work writing, but it is used in the attempt to answer the question "why". What is frequently neglected is the variety of answers that can be given to this question. The answer can refer, for example, to the reasons foster parents give, or to goals which they themselves do not acknowledge or of which they are unaware. Discussion of "motives" for fostering often obscures this difference.

We have all seen in our mind's eye, if not in reality, a list of motives acceptable and unacceptable in foster parents. There is, for example, a traditional suspicion towards those rare but possibly skilful people who seek to implement their income by caring for children. Yet, as the Mundella Report argues, "it is not unreasonable that the foster parents should derive some small advantage from taking the children, for the trouble and anxiety involved in the education of a child is worthy of some remuneration".[2] What is important in such cases is not simply to ascertain the presence of

---

[1] It is important in this respect to consider some of the research on selection of other kinds of "personnel".

See, for example, Kelly, E. L., and Fisher, D. W., *The Prediction of Performance in Clinical Psychology*, 1951. Their evidence suggests that there are fairly strict limitations on the amount of information that people can actually make use of in making predictions. "In retrospect, we cannot help but wonder whether it is unreasonable to expect a human being to function at the extraordinary level of efficiency required by the complex process of predicting behaviour." (p. 201.)

[2] Mundella Committee on Poor Law Schools, C. 8027 (1896), p. 96.

an economic motive, but to question why this particular and hazardous way of supplementing income has been chosen. What is the place of this acknowledged motive in the hierarchy of motives that exist in any personality?

Again, we may look warily upon parents who seem to want a companion for their own child or to fill an otherwise empty life, or upon a wife who requests a foster child because her husband is frequently away from home on business. Yet such motives indicate the direction of further study rather than provide grounds for the rejection of the application. We need to explore with the applicants why, for example, their lives feel empty; is this because they are not able to form satisfying relationships, or because the relationships they have formed neither satisfy their needs nor exhaust their capabilities?

It is not, however, simply a question of discussing the existence of motives. As Towle has pointed out, it is a common fallacy in contemporary social work thinking that "to know the motive is to know the outcome of the course of action".[1] The child care officer has to adopt a dynamic view of motives and to study the likely ways in which foster parents might attempt to achieve their goals and the likely quality of their response towards any help that might be offered by child care workers in the future.

In trying to predict the ways in which foster parents may seek to achieve their goals we will be concerned principally with their flexible response to stresses they may meet in the near future. What we are seeking are people whose motives may be ambiguous and who will be reasonably self-seeking, but whose fostering care will not be exclusively sustained in these terms. If the foster parents expect the child to be a companion to themselves or their own child, are they also likely to allow little or no behaviour that is not in line with that expectation? Will they only value in the foster child his performance as companion, or will other values be allowed expression and recognition? Answers to such questions are, of course, extremely difficult, but they may be found by attempting to study the extent to which the parents have rigidly adhered to other plans in their lives, the extent to which they insist on a child of a particular specification, and how far they can consider and take account of the

---

[1] Towle, C., in discussion following Josslyn, L., "Evaluating Motives of Foster-Parents", *Child Welfare* (*U.S.A.*), Vol. XXXI, No. 2, February, 1952.

needs and problems of others. This can be discovered to some extent in their detailed reactions to the application process; in the way they respond to the "difference" the worker makes in the situation and to the considerations she presents to them, which may well be "different" from those they originally entertained.

The attempt to foresee likely stresses in the future is made by considering what the applicants have asked for, the present structure of the family and the particular foster child for whom the home is sought. The request of the applicants had already been discussed, but some attention will now be paid to the other aids to the anticipation of likely stress. Thinking in terms of stages in the life of a family can be helpful in this context. For example, we may wonder what sort of reactions can be expected from placing an adolescent girl (15) with a man (46) and his wife (45) who have successfully reared two boys (18 and 20), now leaving home. The family has in some ways lost balance by the departure of the boys, will this be restored by placing a girl at a time when the mother may well be deeply concerned with her own declining sexuality and fears of the possible attractive rival?

In thinking of what the child needs and what he can stand, we must endeavour to understand both his history and his present functioning. Here knowledge of stages of development and of his particular ways of present functioning are important. We must avoid stereotypical responses, such as the placement of every adolescent boy in a home which can provide opportunity for reasonable masculine identification. His particular history may indicate that an attempt should be made to involve him first in a warm mothering relationship, which he partially lacked in his early infancy. Yet he may have defended himself very much against acknowledging this need, and it may finally be decided that he should be placed in a home which, though reasonably warm in relationship, allows some distance. What the history of the child should help us to do is to avoid repeating unhealthy patterns of the past. For example, George, an illegitimate boy, was brought up by his mother until the age of seven. The mother then deserts him and he is fostered with a couple in their late fifties; the foster father is in very poor health. A year later the foster father dies, and the child is faced with a repetition of his earlier pathological history when he was the only "man" in the family. The possibility of this happening should certainly have been considered when the application was made.

Perhaps one of the most important impressions that the child care officer inevitably acquires comes from the impact the applicants make upon her and the way they respond to her ways of helping them explore and express their feelings. The worker should consider this to be an important aspect of selection since she has to assess the likely ways in which the foster parents would react to her supervision. As the Curtis Report stated, the applicant should be willing "to further the interests and abilities of the child and *to accept help in doing so*"[1] [my italics]. Clare Britton has stressed the significance of this view in the selection of foster parents: "It is important that the worker chooses people with whom she feels she can establish a good working relationship."[2] It is equally important to keep this feeling free from idiosyncrasy. The applicant's effect on the worker's feelings constitutes important evidence about the sort of person the applicant is (does she, for example, make the worker feel exhausted and empty, overwhelmingly sympathetic or in mutual communication?) When such feelings are positive, the worker may consider herself justified in thinking she can work with this person as a foster parent. If, however, such feelings are unchecked by scrutiny and untried against other evidence the resulting relationship, whilst it is effective and fruitful for the original worker, may well create serious difficulties for her successor. This is a matter of some importance in view of the rapid turnover of child care staff.

These, then, are the areas in which knowledge is required—what do the applicants want, and in what ways will they probably seek this satisfaction? It is useful to consider the stage the family has reached and possible strain in view of the particular foster child's own stage of development and of what he needs and can stand. Finally, the worker will want to know how the applicants are likely to respond to her help. None of this knowledge is easy to acquire, and in some cases it will not be acquired until foster parents and child care officer have had the chance to work together. As Towle has remarked,

"it is not initial motivation that matters as much as capacity for remotivation . . . It would seem to follow that in some instances an

[1] Report of the Care of Children Committee (Curtis), Cmd. 6922, 1946, p. 155.
[2] Britton, C., *op. cit.*

individual's capacity for foster parenthood can be known only through his experience in that role."[1]

Nevertheless, the systematic acquisition of knowledge can begin when contact is first made with the applicants. How can this be done? To turn from the comparatively easy task of listing requirements to the problems of how we begin to acquire knowledge in individual cases is to consider the third aspect of selection, the child care officer's skill.

Skill in Selection

Skill cannot be considered apart from objectives. In preliminary contact with potential foster parents the child care officer has two main objectives. First she should convey to them a realistic and positive idea of what foster parenthood entails. Secondly, she has to investigate a particular home and assess it in the light of the factors considered above. These two objectives are closely connected in the process of the initial interview. For example, the way in which the foster parents respond to the child care officer's explanations of the Department will provide some material for assessing suitability. Do they really hear what she is saying or are they too concerned with stressing their needs? Do they alter this response as the worker helps them to feel secure?

The worker hopes to present to the foster parents a realistic and positive idea of what is entailed in taking into their home the child of other parents, who is the responsibility of the Children's Department. In explaining the way the Department carries out this responsibility she may sometimes talk in general terms of responsibility shared with foster parents, of the part natural parents might play in the situation and so on. In other words, she may try to help prospective foster parents envisage what a future experience may be like. But she and the foster parents are engaging in a present experience which can serve as a model of the kind of help the foster parents might expect in the future. By helping them think about their present feelings as they begin to see the ramifications of their application she demonstrates what a relationship can be like with an officer who has responsibility to both child and foster parent. The officer in the initial interview is assisting the foster parents to

[1] Towle, C., *op. cit.*

reach a reasonable decision; they cannot reach this decision unless she presents them with the reality of fostering.

The worker has also to investigate or to study the home and family. These two words are used to describe the same process; "study" may perhaps be used because of our reluctance to "investigate", but the terms do not matter provided we do not conceal from ourselves that the child care officer needs certain information on certain topics, both facts and feelings about the facts. This information is used to reach a decision on acceptability. Yet the investigation does not simply serve the purpose of the child care officer. She will want to know, for example, the possible repercussions of a foster child on a family and this is also something the foster parents need to think about before they can decide if they wish to proceed with their application.

In studying applications the child care officer is not a free-lance investigator. She has certain duties to fulfil in the course of this study and these can be seen as providing a helpful framework for the process. The Boarding-Out Regulations in fact place a heavy responsibility on the child care officer. Regulation 17 (i) states:

A child shall not be boarded-out unless—

(a) the foster parents and the dwelling where the child will live have been visited by a visitor who is personally acquainted with the child and his needs, or, when that is not practicable, by a visitor who has been fully informed thereof, and the visitor has reported in writing that the sleeping and living accommodation and other domestic conditions at the dwelling are satisfactory and that the household of the foster parents is likely to suit the particular needs of the child;

(b) information has been obtained by a visitor and a written report made by him—

    (i) on the reputation and religious persuasion of the foster parents and their suitability in age, character, temperament and health to have charge of *the* child (my italics);

    (ii) as to whether any member of the foster parents' household is believed to be suffering from any physical or mental illness which might adversely affect the child or to have been convicted of any offence which would render it undesirable that the child should associate with him, and

    (iii) on the number, sex and approximate age of the persons in that household.

Thus although a great part of the decision on suitability rests, of necessity, with the child care officer, she has defined responsibilities to secure information on certain points. Some of the sources of information (*e.g.*, police and doctors) will be of help on certain specific issues, such as the existence or otherwise of a criminal record that would adversely effect the child. On the whole, however, the larger the question the less useful the answer. Thus references about the foster parents' "character" and "reputation" are probably the least useful of the sources of information beyond the interview with the applicant. As a worker for the C.O.S. remarked early in this century: "To go to people about whom we know nothing in order to ask them about people concerning whom they know nothing (or at any rate nothing that is *ad rem*) is not a very fruitful proceeding."[1] Many references are mere certificates of competence for foster parenthood signed by people who know little or nothing of what foster parenthood entails. There will, of course, be exceptions, but the usual references tell us at best the kind of person the applicants know, and at worst are of no use at all. Yet the duty to collect certain defined information helps the child care officer to study the way in which applicants respond to these necessary conditions of the application. It should be noted also that the use of references is easily accepted by applicants as a way of obtaining reports that may or may not be completely favourable.

There is some controversy in the field of child care over the point at which details of a particular child are discussed with prospective applicants. Gordon, for example, in a well-known American text, argues that

> "Applicants should have made their decision, and the agency should have accepted their home, before the caseworker discusses a specific child with them ... Deciding to withdraw may seem (to the foster mother) like rejecting the child, or she may have the mistaken idea that she can be of service only by accepting a specific child who, for very valid reasons, she may not feel able to take."[2]

In England, however, it has become quite usual practice to advertise for foster homes for particular children, and emphasis has not been placed on helping the foster parents to reach a general decision about themselves as foster parents, partly because of the great pressure on Children's Departments to foster children and the real shortage of foster homes. Presenting the picture of an actual child

---

[1] M.W.G., "What do we Mean by Enquiry?", *Charity Organization Review*, January, 1941.
[2] Gordon, H., *op. cit.*, p. 138.

to prospective parents does help to avoid too much generality, and seems to be particularly helpful for parents who do not feel at home with concepts and generalizations. Yet it is important to bear in mind questions of confidentiality. There is certainly information about individual children which should not be revealed until the applicants have been accepted as foster parents.

Three Situations

Three brief extracts from initial interviews with foster parents will now be examined in order to illustrate some of the generalizations about skill discussed above. Only selected aspects of the cases will be considered.

> I. Mrs. A. then asked about our rules. She had learnt that the Council (well, not the Council exactly, but I would know what she meant) give strict instructions to the parents about times of children coming in and all that. I said we did not have rules like that; if we trusted a foster parent with a child we would trust her to care for him like one of her own and to let the child care officer know if any difficulties did develop. I mentioned some of the difficulties that might arise (visits of parents, testing-out by the child, etc.) and how difficult it was for foster parents if the child had to be returned to the natural parents. Mrs. A. said she was much more concerned about what the child might feel. I asked if she had difficulties with bringing up her own children.

In this case the applicant shows that she has not a very clear picture of the structure of the Children's Department, and some clarification could have been given. Of more importance, however, is the difficulty Mrs. A. expresses about rules and possibly about supervision. This could have been explored in terms of her feelings about sharing responsibility for a child. Mrs. A. mentions a specific ruling and it may be useful to consider in the light of other material if this is the only sphere in which "rules" bother her. Her difficulties are, however, discussed by the worker in general terms (*e.g.*, the sort of difficulties foster mothers in general face). Moreover, when Mrs. A. again returns to the specific (she would be worried about what the child would feel) the worker turns the discussion away to difficulties Mrs. A. might have had with her own children. This is a rather generalized question and one that might rouse considerable defensiveness on her part.

> II. (*From a second interview when the worker calls to see the father.*)
>
> Father was busy dressing one of the children; he ignored me, taking refuge in his task and in the T.V. When the child was dressed I asked

him what he felt about his wife's idea (of taking a foster child): "If my wife decides to go in for this, it's up to her. After all, she will do all the work." I said we were anxious that they should be quite united in their plan and he repeated it was up to her. I turned to Mrs. B. and said her husband did not seem very keen on her idea. She replied that they never argued and he would be behind her whatever she did, as long as it wasn't too bad. I asked Mr. B. again what he really thought and he said he didn't want to take a baby. She commented that that was more than he had ever told her and he said he didn't want her pushing prams up all those hills again. They can now take all the family on the 'bus without push chairs and he did not want to go back to them. Mrs. B. commented that he had never pushed a pram in his life and he replied "No! and I don't want to start now". He then said heavily, "Now what does this really involve?" I said it meant taking a child into the home to live as one of the family. "Agreed, but what about people coming in? I am not going to have people coming in and saying 'You must not do this or you must not do that, or this child hasn't enough calories or sunshine or something'." I explained that people would be calling and I suggested the parents should talk to a foster mother who lived nearby.

The worker is clearly correct in trying to press Mr. B. about his feelings in regard to fostering, despite his initial evasion. She poses the problem to Mrs. B. as one of disagreement—"your husband does not seem very keen on the idea". Yet she had the opportunity later in the interview to further her knowledge of the marital relationship by presenting the problem to the couple as a joint problem. If she had said something like "you both have strong feelings about this. It is rather like starting the family again. How do you feel about this?" it would have been possible for her to see how the parents reacted to this opportunity of discussing a problem presented as a joint difficulty.

In assessing the reaction of Mr. B. to the idea of fostering, the worker has to consider also the hostility directed towards her, directly and indirectly, by Mr. B. In the interview she responds with persistent interest in the expression of his point of view and by stating the realities of supervision (*e.g.*, people will call). She also offers the possibility of reassurance through a third party. It would also have been useful if she had tried to discover the meaning of Mr. B.'s feelings about officials, etc., possibly by a reference to what he felt about her present "intrusion". This would have shown Mr. B. that the worker recognized some of his feelings towards her in the present and helped to form a more precise idea of how far he could co-operate in supervision.

III. Visited Mr. and Mrs. C.; Mrs. C. was in the middle of washing. Apologized for the untimely call, but said I had called about her application for John (subject of the advertisement). Mrs. C. said she would like me to stay and discuss the matter none-the-less. I told Mrs. C. I would prefer to call again when her husband was at home and had really only dropped in to make an appointment. She was not to be deterred; said she'd been hoping someone would come as she was "fair bursting for news" and could I stay for a cup of coffee and tell her something about the "laddy". I apologized and said I had another appointment but would call that evening. This was agreed.

Visited that evening. Introduced myself and thanked them for their application. As Mrs. C. seemed enthusiastic to conduct the interview I felt it would be fruitful to let her talk. Mr. C. appeared a quiet, pleasant man content to let his wife take the initiative. Mrs. C. said they had been very thrilled when the saw the advertisement, as it seemed to be the "answer to prayer". She said that her daughter had just emigrated to Canada taking her two children, both boys, aged three and five with her. Apparently, they had lived with the C.'s ever since their marriage and although the C.'s had a son, Philip (aged 19) and another daughter, married and living away, they felt this departure acutely. Mrs. C. complained that the house seemed "dead" and that she couldn't acclimatize to so much time on her hands. Speaking also for Mr. C. she said "we just feel lost". I suggested to Mr. C., in an attempt to draw him into the conversation, that the house must seem very quiet and peaceful now—he replied "Yes, it does".

Halted Mrs. C.'s soliloquy at this stage and said that before further discussion perhaps I could take a few particulars from them; these are always required by the Children's Committee when they consider an application for a foster child. For once, Mr. C. replied, and said "Aye, certainly you have your job to do." I apologized for the rather personal content of the questions, but said I was sure they understood that we had to take the responsibility of finding homes for children very seriously, and unless we had some information about the kind of people applying for foster children we could not hope to help the child to get the right placement, or the foster parents to get the type of child best suited to their needs. Mrs. C. interrupted here and said it was the "laddy" she wanted—he was just the "right" age and she was used to boys—she thought they were more affectionate than girls "for all their wicked ways". At this Mr. C. gave an enigmatic laugh and said "boys will be boys". Particulars taken.

It is easy for initial interviews to develop at cross-purposes, the applicant wanting a particular child (*e.g.*, Mrs. C.) and the child care officer seeking information to assess the request. Part of this difficulty may be overcome if the worker herself does not feel bound to treat every first interview with applicants as an application, but rather as an interview with the purpose of deciding whether or not the prospective foster parents will make a firm application. This may seem unrealistic and wishful, in view of the pressure of work in

Departments, but time spent at the initial stage may save much time and possible failure later and helps the worker follow more securely the process of the application.

It is clear that in the case of Mrs. C. there is difficulty in establishing the common purpose of meeting to discuss the implications and meaning of their application. The worker rightly reveals to Mrs. C. some of the reality of supervision by showing the necessity for appointments and the interest of the Department in both parents. She seems to feel pressure from Mrs. C. in their first encounter, and she might have felt more at ease and at the same time given Mrs. C. encouragement to think about a common purpose if she had said something like:— "I can see that you feel very excited about the possibility and I know waiting will seem very annoying" (or "difficult"). It would also probably have helped if the questions had been introduced rather more as a means of safeguarding the interests of the applicants and perhaps less as an intrusion on privacy in the interest of the child. In this way the worker would have presented herself as someone concerned for both foster parents and child.

Communication between child care worker and applicant is facilitated largely by the means used in casework and many other relationships. Workers try to ask questions that help people to expand what has previously been expressed and that seem unlikely to rouse defensiveness. Thus, the worker with Mr. C., correctly wishing to test what kind of contribution Mrs. C. will allow him to make and to discover what he feels about the situation, asks a question but almost in the same words as Mrs. C. has previously used. A more enabling question would have been "I wonder what you find you miss most, Mr. C.?"

Workers try also to help people to express what particular statements mean to them in terms of their own experience. It would have been useful to discover what Mrs. C. meant by "the wicked ways" of young boys. One of the most useful aids to communication is to follow as closely as possible the movement of an interview, not simply the subjects discussed, but the feelings expressed in this discussion. Yet in this case the worker cuts across both subject and feeling. For example, she cuts across Mrs. C.'s discussion of how she feels now her children have gone and this is an important area for exploration.

Rejection

Perhaps because it is one of the most difficult aspects of the selection of foster parents, discussion of rejecting prospective parents has been delayed until this point. Because it is painful to reject, especially when the applicants have offered themselves, in some senses as parents, it is often tempting to deal with rejected applications speedily and as routine. Pressure of work helps us to do this with a greater feeling of justification. Another way of dealing with this problem is to attempt to avoid the issue by telling applicants that they will be placed on a waiting-list. This sometimes results in a series of abortive calls from the applicants asking, from time to time, if a suitable child has been found. Such a way of dealing with the problem is unsatisfactory and often painful for both applicant and officer. As social workers and as administrators, child care officers should give more attention to this problem. As social workers they believe that people have intrinsic value, and should not be used exclusively as a means to an end. As administrators, they should be conscious of the likely effects of the inconsiderate treatment of applicants on the reputation of their foster care programme.

Ideally, of course, the worker hopes to help unsuitable applicants to decide to withdraw themselves. Sometimes this can be achieved. Where it cannot, the worker has to decide whether the applicant should be told the reason for rejection or not. Some Departments never give reasons; some may feel reasons would be too damaging to the applicants themselves. It is perhaps possible more often than we imagine to share with the parents at least some of the reasons why their application has been refused. This is often done more effectively by visit than letter. A visit shows that the applicant is valued, that it has been considered worthwhile to explain the reasons for refusal personally. To some applicants, the reasons can be explained frankly. For others, this would be too damaging, and the refusal can perhaps be conveyed in terms of some factor in the material environment, such as distance from school, etc. If we have considered the applications carefully and imaginatively, we can reject some offers with confidence that our action is in the best interest of both applicants and child. In communicating this confidence in a right decision, we are enabled to reject not guiltily and hurriedly, but naturally and with consideration.

CHAPTER 6

FOSTER PARENTS AND THE CHILD CARE OFFICER (2)

> "The choice of a home is no doubt a matter of the
> highest importance ... But selection is not the only
> thing necessary; supervision should come afterwards,
> and it is neither safe nor right to trust to even the best
> selected foster parents."
>
> MASON[1]

IN this chapter an attempt will be made to characterize some of the
problems that arise in the foster home and to suggest ways in which
the child care officer helps foster parents to deal with them. The
division between the work of selection and the work of help
(emphasized by the division of subject matter between these two
chapters), is basically a matter of convenience. The knowledge the
worker acquires for purposes of selection must serve also as a basis
for help if the home is selected; the way in which the worker helps
foster parents over difficulties is an expansion of the means she
used to help them as applicants.

Problems

This chapter emphasizes the place of relationships both in the
understanding and the management of problems in foster care. Such
problems are commonly formulated in terms of a list of difficulties
ranging from intolerable behaviour in the child (*e.g.*, bed-wetting,
stealing, unresponsiveness to affection) to apparently minor complaints about a detail of Children's Department policy (*e.g.*, the
method of paying the allowance). A list of such symptoms is,
however, less helpful than the attempt to see the problem in terms
of the relationships between foster mother, child and child care
officer. A useful way of grouping problems is to consider them as:
(*a*) problems of adequacy; (*b*) problems of rivalry and (*c*) problems
of control.

[1] 21 Local Government Board, 1891/2, p. 195.

(a) *Adequacy.*—Foster parents offer a service; they present the capable and affectionate part of themselves. They risk failure, and bad behaviour on the part of the child may often seem to be failure. For some foster parents this thought may be so difficult to face that they delay expressing their worry about such behaviour until they are caught up in a tangled relationship with the child. Problems of adequacy are not usually fully met by simple explanation. Take, for example, the following incident:—

> Roger, aged 6½, cries very easily and frequently. This upsets the foster parents, who say that neighbours have complained about the crying. The worker explains that Roger has had a very unhappy life and needs all the affection they can give. The parents say they are worried about his bed-wetting, and the worker says that if Roger has time to settle she is sure this will make a difference.

This brief extract shows how vulnerable foster parents are in terms of the projection from neighbours and others of the image of the wicked step-parent. In order to deal with this projection and the foster parents' own possible feelings that their love is insufficient, it is not enough to reiterate the child's need. The worker should begin to help the foster parents by showing that she can understand (or is trying to understand) how they must feel in the face of apparent failure.

A second extract shows how a child care officer attempted to deal with a similar problem in a different way. This is an extract from the case of Betty, who has already been discussed in Chapter Four.

> 28.4.52. Betty's tendency to romance reached a peak last week when a neighbour told the Walkers that Betty said that Mr. Walker had thrashed her. The foster parents felt very hurt about this, and Betty cried bitterly when they told her of the story. The worker, after some discussion with the Walkers, managed to persuade them that Betty was only behaving thoughtlessly and did not realize the significance of what she was saying. The worker assured them of her confidence in them. On the insistence of the foster parents the worker saw Betty, who seemed shaken that the child care officer had been sent for. She suggested that Betty be encouraged in games of fantasy and the telling of stories, say at bedtime, which would eliminate the necessity for sensationalism and provide an outlet for this capacity of hers.

Here the worker is anxious to preserve this placement, in which Betty seems to be settling well. So she "persuades" the foster parents that Betty is behaving thoughtlessly. Yet this is probably not so.

The worker knows that Mr. Walker shows less inclination to give Betty up at times of difficulty than his wife. Is there some special relationship between Mr. Walker and Betty that leads Betty to make her allegations? Does she want to be punished? Is punishment of special significance for her in her relationship with Mr. Walker? Whatever the situation, Betty is saying something about her relationship with Mr. Walker, and the child care officer might well have considered it appropriate to help the Walkers see something, or rather discover something, of any problem she might be facing. Obviously, the possible sexual elements in this situation would not be discussed, but the foster parents might be helped to wonder why she invents this particular story. They could be helped to think about this if they are assured of the worker's confidence. It is doubtful how far specific (and rather odd-sounding) suggestions about what to do will take the place of this other kind of help. The suggestion that Betty be encouraged to tell stories and romance must surely serve only to convince the foster parents that the worker does not appreciate their desire to control this aspect of Betty's behaviour. The child care officer is not a missionary for advanced child care practice. She is someone who tries to understand problems and she shows people that she does so understand or at least tries to.

(b) *Rivalry.*—So much sharing is implicit in the fostering situation that rivalry and jealousy can frequently be seen. Many foster parents find it very hard to tolerate the visits of natural parents or those of their foster child to a former foster home or to his natural parents. This may seem to endanger the patient work of weeks. It is sometimes hard to accept the fact that in spite of all the foster parents' giving, the child still has love for his parents. Rivalry can also develop between the foster parents over the child, or between the foster child and natural children or foster parents and child care worker. Foster parents may, for example, envy all the good things the Children's Department does for the foster child, compared to their own fate or that of their natural children. One foster mother remarked to her worker: "I'm always telling her the Committee have been very good to her and she's a lot to be grateful for. In fact she's more clothes than our Jean."

An example of the difficulty foster parents often have in sharing the foster child with members of his natural family can be found in the case of George (born 20.4.51).

13.10.54. Home visit to Mrs. Reginald (24) who has had George as a foster child since May, 1954. She has a daughter, Felicity, of 2 years. She reports that George is making progress and his speech is gradually improving. He has been difficult recently about asking for his potty. The officer suggests that he might be seeking attention by his behaviour, possibly because of his unsettled infancy. George makes a great fuss of Mr. Reginald, says the foster mother, and when he is around she is almost ignored. Mrs. Reginald said she was a little hurt and worried by this, and the child care officer tells her that it is a frequent and natural occurrence. The foster mother says that George was taken to see his brother, Peter, the other day, but she is worried in case his visits make Peter unhappy because he is still in a Children's Home. The worker explains that he would be more unhappy if he felt forgotten.

3.12.54. . . . Mrs. Reginald has seen the advertisement for Peter for a foster home and seems distressed by her inability to do anything for him. She thinks, however, that George will become unsettled by his visits to Peter, and shows reluctance in discussing this with the worker. She goes to great length to maintain a scrupulous equality between her own daughter and George.

It seems that this foster mother has problems about sharing. She is probably denying some of the difference in her feeling for George, if she is so scrupulous in maintaining equality, and she shows some difficulty in sharing George with her husband. It looks as if her feelings about George visiting his brother is partly due to her inability to offer a home for the latter and partly perhaps to fear that she will have to share George with his brother. More exact dimensions of her problem would be obtained if the worker had given more attention to the foster mother's feelings, rather than emphasizing the normality of George's behaviour in view of his past.

The problems implicit in sharing have, of course, been emphasized by recent changes in child care policy. The view that the "fresh start is no longer possible" and that the family ties of children in care should be preserved and developed has undoubtedly created difficulties in child care work. At times parents must seem "impossible" and the work of maintaining contact between them and their children unavailing. Yet what evidence we have suggests that such contact is important. Weinstein, for example, has shown that this has a significant influence on the child's adjustment to the foster home.[1]

(c) *Control.*—There are special problems associated with controlling other people's children. Foster parents may sometimes feel

[1] Weinstein, E. A., *The Self-Image of the Foster Child*, 1960.

guilty about caring for another's child (because they fear they are depriving the natural parent of his love) and this may be complicated by the child's difficult behaviour. Foster children frequently behave in ways which threaten the foster parents' solutions of their own earlier conflicts and problems. The sexual, aggressive and demanding behaviour of foster children may often present foster parents with the problem of re-establishing control over these impulses in themselves. The case of Mrs. C. (given later) illustrates this kind of problem.

In many cases, of course, these problems of adequacy, rivalry and control are combined. The following is a short extract from a case presenting them all in varying degrees.

> The child care officer visited Mrs. Reed after Andrew (aged 5 years, and in care almost from birth) had spent a week-end with the family as a prospective foster child. The Reeds were both in their early thirties and had a son of their own, Richard, aged four. Mrs. Reed gave the following account of the week-end:
>
> After breakfast Andrew and Richard played with toys, but Andrew wanted the toys Richard played with and lost his temper when Richard would not surrender them. During the morning Andrew was sent out to play in the garden, but he was found throwing earth at next door's dog and, later, wandering into people's houses. He was then put in the spare room to play with Richard. On hearing the sound of broken glass, Mrs. Reed went upstairs and found Andrew standing with a spanner in his hand. Mr. Reed asked Richard if he had broken the window, but he denied it. Mr. Reed smacked him. He asked Andrew, who said nothing. Mr. Reed "tapped" Andrew a couple of times, but received no response; Andrew just stood and sulked. After this, they decided they would take Andrew back to the children's home. When Mr. Reed left him he cried for the first time. This surprised the Reeds, who had thought he was incapable of tears.
>
> Mrs. Reed said they had found it difficult to treat the children equally, and were afraid they were tending to be unfair to their own son. They were very emphatic that no discrimination should be shown. Mrs. Reed said she would have Andrew on one knee and Richard on the other and when Mr. Reed kissed Richard she would remind him to kiss Andrew also. However they had decided they could not keep him. He had seemed a very pleasant child in the nursery, but now they felt they knew him better. His naughtiness seemed more than ordinary naughtiness, and Mrs. Reed was worried about his background and the possible effect on her own son. Mr. Reed still wanted to take Andrew out and had been willing to keep him a little longer, but Mrs. Reed felt she could not always be watching him.

This extract emphasizes the importance of preparing the foster parents for the anticipated behaviour of the child, whether it is likely to be good or bad. Such preparation helps the parents to

8

form some idea of how far they are adjusting to the child and the child to them. To give insufficient preparation is to leave them surprised and anxious, and to make them feel cheated by the worker or by the child or both. Of course, no preparation before an event is ever the same as experience of the event, but child care workers must be sure that they have prepared the foster home as fully as they can. In the case of Andrew, such preparation would have concentrated on his likely behaviour towards the foster parents and Richard. In view of the risk of placing a foster child of the same age and sex as the natural child of the foster parents, great care should have been exercised in order to ascertain that there were strong positive compensating features in the home.

In the case of the Reeds it is clear that there is considerable concern about possible rivalry, and what amounts to a denial of difference, for example, in the case of punishment by Mr. Reed. In preparing these foster parents or in discussing the present break-down, some recognition by the worker of the fact that it is natural to feel differently towards a foster child whom one has recently met would have been helpful.

Ways of Helping

If it is useful to characterize problems in the context of a relation-ship, it also is helpful to consider relationships as a means of helping foster parents with these problems. Ways of helping will be con-sidered under the following headings (i) the worker's own attitudes (ii) the relationship between worker and foster parents. An attempt will then be made to illustrate ways of handling this relationship by extracts from interviews with foster parents, and, finally, with a full length record of work with one foster home.

(i) *The Worker's Own Attitude.*—Strictly speaking, this can hardly be classed as a *way* of helping. Yet, it is often stated that the social worker helps as much by what she is as by what she does. This can perhaps become an unfortunate division between "being" some-body and doing something. We show what we are by the way in which we do things; we do not, as it were, form a relationship by "being" a particular sort of person and then go out to "do" things for the client or *vice versa*. As long, however, as this is understood it is profitable to consider separately such phenomena as the worker's own attitudes.

The importance of these attitudes is by now axiomatic in social work, but we need to keep the notion vividly before us, to consider and re-consider the ways in which our attitudes might affect the relationships we establish in Child Care work. It is not simply that particular behaviour (*e.g.*, bullying, lying, etc.) may disturb our own defences against impulses of the same kind, but that in the field of Child Care there exist special seductions for the unwary or negligent worker.

The child care worker has to come to terms with both her legally sanctioned power (her authority by means of statutory obligations) and the forceful position in which she is placed by the fantasy of both parents and children. Relationships with foster parents are regulated not simply by the problems that may find expression or the needs of foster parents, but by statutory regulation. The main framework of supervision of foster homes is laid down in Home Office Regulations and in the practice of individual Departments. The Regulations direct the child care officer to the consideration of certain facts and to the formation of a judgment upon them. Regulation 9 instructs that

> "Whenever, in pursuance of these Regulations, a visitor sees a child who is boarded out he shall after considering the welfare, health, conduct and progress of the child and any complaint made by or concerning him, make a written report about the child, and whenever a visitor so visits the dwelling of foster parents he shall make a written report about its condition."

These reports are part of an attempt "to exclude unpremeditated or casual meetings"[1] and serve as the basis for a review of the "the welfare, conduct, health and progress of every child who is boarded out" at specified intervals (s. 22). There is no specific regulation enforcing a review of religious upbringing, but, since foster parents have to undertake that the foster child will be brought up in his religious persuasion it is presumably expected that some check will be made from time to time. This question of religious upbringing is, however, one of considerable difficulty in the Service, and the unsatisfactory nature of the regulations is symptomatic of our confused feeling on the subject. This difficulty will be considered in Chapter Eight.

On the whole, however, the regulations maintain clear minimum standards of supervision, and ensure not only that the foster parent

---

[1] Memorandum on the Boarding-Out of Children Regulations, 1955, para 25.

is helped (*e.g.*, to voice complaint) but also that the Department has information about current developments in the child's life, and thus can judge how far the aims set in regard to each individual child are being realized. The regulations help in securing certain purposes of the Department, but for some workers they sometimes constitute a difficulty. These workers may not feel at ease in "inspecting" the homes of applicants, or in enquiring about the religious observances of children or parent. Unless they have come to terms with their own feelings about the statutory regulations that describe the basic minimum of their work, they will convey to the foster parents their own misgiving and uneasiness, and lose a valuable support in their work. It is this that gives first interviews so much of their importance; here the worker must begin to convey the purpose and the nature of supervision and its framework of regulation.

The child care officer is often seen by foster and natural parents and by children as someone who has great power. She will sometimes have projected on to her the images of the good or of the bad mother and of the all-wise expert. She is seen as having the power to give and the power to take away children, someone who judges the adequacy of children and parents. It is important that the worker's own feelings are not too uneasy in the presence of such images. The worker will also need to consider how far she may see herself as a foster parent or a child, how far over-grateful to foster, or punitive to natural, parents. It is not difficult in child care work to use either foster or natural parents merely as the environment of the child.

Emphasis on the child at the expense of the adults around him sometimes appears in the way child care officers regard the causes of foster home breakdown. Sometimes the cause of breakdown seems to be found exclusively in the behaviour or in the personality disturbance of the foster parents. The child, in this context, is seen as a powerless pawn moved hither and thither by the psychopathology of foster parents. A more helpful approach is to consider the relationship between child and significant adults as essentially interacting, so that each partner is seen as contributing to the gradually established network of feeling. When faced with a problem in fostering, it is always important to see if this is part of a pattern of behaviour visible, in outlines more or less clear, in the past. It may be that the particular child we are trying to help has a need to repeat the past, and goes through life managing to provoke situations that resemble an original injurious incident in a significant relationship. Of course, we must not swing from blaming foster parents to blaming children; some foster parents are particularly vulnerable to some kinds of problem. The important factors to consider are the past and present relationships of both foster parent and foster child.

(ii) *The Relationship between Worker and Foster Parents.*—There is no simple way of describing this relationship. Clare Britton has suggested that "it is a composite one—supportive, educational and supervisory—with emphasis on each of the functions as need arises, but mostly with all three being carried out simultaneously".[1] Some writers have spoken of the relationship as a casework relationship. Others have suggested that the foster mother "cannot be a client and a successful foster mother both".[2] Others again have drawn analogies with the situation of casework supervision. However, analogies break down at some point. What can be said about the relationship —its basis and its purpose?

In the first place it must in general be agreed that applicants do not come to the placement agency (statutory or voluntary) with a problem. There is, in other words, no warrant for a worker–client relationship. Glickman, however, maintains a different view. She has stated that it can probably be assumed that the foster parents have asked for a child as an indirect way of requesting help for themselves. On this assumption, she suggests that in certain rare instances the placement worker may engage in "direct treatment of the underlying problems within the foster family".[3] (It is, incidentally, worth noting that Glickman's term "intensive treatment" may perhaps give a misleading impression, to judge from the example she gives, which seems to consist mainly of sympathetic listening on the part of the worker.) A treatment approach to the supervision of foster homes is not, it is thought, the most helpful. The child care officer and the applicants come together to satisfy the needs of child and of the applicants as prospective foster parents. The relationship with foster parents has as its purpose the maintenance and development of this mutual satisfaction, and for this purpose study,

[1] Britton, C., *op. cit.*
[2] Cole, L. C., "The Triangle in Child Placement", *Social Service Review*, June, 1951.
[3] Glickman, E., *op. cit.*, p. 224.

an enabling relationship and specific support continue all the time.

Yet a realistic view of the work of the child care officer must take account of the ease with which foster mothers, in particular, begin to respond to the interest of a regular and sympathetic visitor and to discuss, for example, their marital problems. This situation demands casework skill, if the limits of the officer's work are to be defined with the foster parents without leading them to feel rejected. It would, in general, be unfortunate if it was insisted so rigidly that foster parents were not clients that no casework skills were used, leaving the foster parents high and dry, with neither the satisfaction of recognition as colleagues nor the skilled help due to clients.

Take, for example, the following extract from an interview in which the foster mother asks for advice about her foster child:

> Doreen, (7), will not go out to play, but just sits at home and reads. She has recently been stealing money from the foster father. The foster mother has tried sending her to bed, but this didn't stop it. What should she do next? Should she stop her pocket money?

This situation cannot be met adequately by giving specific advice or by listing possible alternative courses of action. This is partly because there simply is no answer to the problem in these terms; very often no one could know what the foster mother should do in any detail. Rather than acknowledge this to the mother, however, and possibly increase her feelings of helplessness, the child care officer may say something like: "Yes, it is puzzling (or 'worrying', etc.); let us try and work it out together. I wonder why she does this . . . I'm sure there's something we shall find that will be helpful." This is a better approach than to begin: "Have you tried . . ."

In the situation we are considering a short-stay baby had recently been placed in the home, and in the discussion of Doreen's difficulty the child care officer tried to get the mother to see the possible connection. The mother denies any connection of this kind, insisting that she has "done all the things you're supposed to do when a new baby arrives". This shows that the direct approach of suggesting possibilities of jealousy and rivalry arouses too much defensiveness in the mother and that she has difficulty—possibly because of guilt—in recognizing that her handling might have contributed to the problem. Instead, the worker might proceed by expressing some understanding of the mother's worry, and possibly how easy it seems to her for people to lay down lists of things she should do.

It is suggested that this incident illustrates the ways in which casework skills of helping people to explore the meaning of a problem and of recognizing resistances to such an exploration can be used to help foster parents.

In general, work with foster parents can be described as help given through a professional relationship in maintaining and extending the satisfaction of the needs of foster parents and children, and in solving particular problems that arise between the Children's Department, the child, the natural and the foster parents. The worker will need to understand the emotional significance both of her own relationship with the foster parents and of the problems they encounter. It may well be that the relationship reiterates other relationships (particularly in view of the powerful images which, as we have seen, may be projected on to the worker), but she will handle these indirectly. There are two ways in which this indirect management will most probably be carried out; by comment of a general kind (*e.g.*, "It is hard to feel someone comes and seems always to be on the side of the child") and the worker's attitude (*e.g.*, her continued interest and acceptance of the foster parents). Problems, on the other hand, cannot usually be satisfactorily handled in an indirect manner. They should be dealt with more specifically, and the worker will attempt to discover their emotional meaning for the foster parents, but in terms of present reality rather than as echoes of problems in the foster parents' childhood past. Thus, in the case of Doreen's foster mother, just quoted, emphasis should be placed not on discovering what stealing means to her in terms of possible childhood experience, but of her present position as a foster parent struggling with an aggravating problem, needing, for example, to come to a decision on how she should react to the child.

Aspects of the handling of the relationship will now be illustrated by four extracts from interviews with foster parents.

I. The worker is concerned with the feelings of two boys, 9 and 11, fostered with a widow of 62, about their mentally-ill mother. He decides to work with the children on this problem, but first discusses it with the foster mother. The worker makes this decision because of his concern at Mrs. A.'s own "basic fear of mental illness".

"I mentioned that sometimes children will want to talk to an outsider, because if they keep talking to their foster mother about their own parents, they may have a feeling of hurting her. On occasions they may feel more free to talk to an outsider. I told Mrs. A. that I would try to explain their mother's illness and why she was unable to look after them. It helped children to hear the same thing from different people, and it would take some of the pressure off the foster mother."

In this case, the worker had previously noted that Mrs. A. might herself have fears of mental illness, but these are not discussed with her. It might have been possible to help Mrs. A. to express some of the more general fears concerning madness by discussing them as the kind of ideas we usually have. This would have been relevant to the problem in hand. However, the worker decides to supplement the help the foster mother has given the children, and discusses the reasons for doing this with her. This is important, not simply because of courtesy or the fact that to proceed without the permission and understanding of foster parents rarely succeeds, but because of what the discussion accomplishes within the relationship in helping Mrs. A. to feel at one with the worker. If Mrs. A. can be encouraged to feel identified with the worker's unanxious approach to the problem, it is likely that her own fears will be to some extent reduced. Mrs. A.'s fear of mental illness would have been aggravated if the problem had been taken completely out of her hands, and her sense of adequacy would certainly have been threatened. Instead, the worker explains what he hoped to do and why, and shows Mrs A. that he sees something of the difficulty and is not overwhelmed by it nor afraid to do something about it.

> II. I called to see Mrs. B. (foster mother of a 14 year old girl). She said she was worried about the girl. Could I call back later and discuss it when Mr. B. was at home? I said that unfortunately I could not. Mrs. B. said they had dinner at seven; she had lost contact with her friends since she married and it would be nice to entertain. I said I had a number of evening visits, and did not think I could call at seven. Mrs. B. said would it be a nice change for me to eat out?

This is a difficult situation, about which questions are easier to find than answers. Why does Mrs. B. wish to turn this into a social evening? Why does she want to give this meal to the worker? To gain attention or control, or to form a relationship to meet the need for companionship, to offer restitution for hostile wishes or as a way of asking for help? The problem is to understand which of these motives is uppermost and to recognize this with Mrs. B., at the same time avoiding rejection. What seems to be inhibiting the worker in this case is a stereotypical view of what should and should not be allowed in a professional relationship. If she feels that Mrs. B. can only ask for help by way of the invitation and that her need is acute, then the worker should probably accept. If she decides that Mrs. B. really wants to ensure that she has time in which she can really explain her problem and feels that other mothers get more time than she does it might be possible to deal with this in the following way:

"It is very kind of you to invite me; I appreciate the offer. I do want to understand the problem you have with (the child). I can come and discuss this at . . . The fact is I have to visit a number of homes. Perhaps you sometimes feel it's alright my coming and going while you have the day-to-day problems of the care of the children", etc. The approach conveyed in this way implicitly keeps the discussion centred on why the worker calls without directly saying to Mrs. B. that she wishes to make the relationship social. It endeavours to present the reality of the officer's limited time while recognizing some of the resentment this might arouse. It gives assurance of the worker's willingness to understand, and makes a definite time available for the mother in the near future.

> III. Mrs. C. said she was very worried about Sandra's lying (Sandra is a girl of 9). She knew that when she (Mrs. C.) was young, before they had all these experts, children would be sent to bed for a week with no tea. The worker wondered why a week, and Mrs. C. said this had been her punishment the only time in her life she had told a lie. The worker asked how long Sandra's lying had been going on. Mrs. C. replied by saying how much she hated lies; one didn't know where one was. The worker suggested that many children, especially children with an unhappy background, often went through a phase of lying.

This is a complex situation, in which Mrs. C. appears to be expressing hostility towards the "expert" and may have become involved in dealing with her own problem about lies and lying through Sandra. The worker clearly saw that there was something "odd" about Mrs. C.'s very specific statement of "sent to bed for a week" and fruitfully asks Mrs. C. about this. This might have been further discussed in terms of what Mrs. C. felt about it, but not of what the lying was about (since this would have made the worker seem even more of a questioning parent). It may be that the worker's attempt to help Mrs. C. conveyed an implicit understanding of Mrs. C.'s lying as a child (it is as if she said this lying is something that can be traced to unhappiness and is not something to be condemned). Yet her remark is really based on the assumption that Mrs. C. is concerned with the normality of the behaviour in question. Expressions of opinion about the reactions of most adolescents, most deprived children and so on are effective only if the worker has discovered that the parent is troubled about whether the behaviour in question is normal (*i.e.*, usual) or not. In the case of Mrs. C. this seems a premature judgement. Mrs. C. is likely to be concerned with the behaviour as abnormal in the sense of wrong. The worker should in this case aim at recognizing the strength of feeling ("There is something you feel very strongly about" or "something your parents felt strongly about"); indicating by her attitude that she is not shocked into inactivity and still wants to help.

> IV. Home visit, in response to a 'phone call, to the Misses Bartram (53 and 48). Four months ago Jean was boarded with them (aged 12). They refused to keep her because they had learnt all about her family and were very angry with the child care officer for not disclosing this. The child care officer said that it was the first she had heard of it, but doubted if the Misses Bartram believed her. Before this they had seen Jean's behaviour as being entirely the result of living in an institution, but they now saw it entirely in terms of inherent madness and they regarded the situation as hopeless. They also saw Jean as subnormal in intelligence, in spite of the officer's numerous protestations that school reports spoke of her as normal. The officer promised to meet Jean and talk to her about her disobedience. The Misses Bartram said the officer would not persuade them to keep Jean.

The outlook in this case does not appear hopeful. The foster mothers seem to think in rigid terms (the problem is either the effect of institutional life or of inherited insanity) and it is doubtful how far, with such a viewpoint, they could do anything but "rescue" a victim of circumstance or reject an impossibly damaged child. However, in this predicament the worker could usefully have concentrated on some explanation and clarification of her side of this situation, in which they feel cheated and hopeless. The foster mothers seem to think, judging from the last sentence of the interview, that the worker comes exclusively for the sake of the child. More sympathetic and extended attention paid to their feelings of anger and despair would have shown them that this was not the case. It is natural for the worker to feel criticized and attacked in situations like this, but these foster mothers are not ready to listen to her explanation of the "real" facts (*e.g.*, school reports) until some recognition has been given to their feelings as expressed in the interview.

In this discussion of work with foster parents after selection emphasis has been placed on the problems, but there is important work to be done even when there seems to be no problem. The case of Mrs. C. illustrates the feeling some foster parents have that the worker is concerned only with troubles. The relationship between foster parents and worker is as important in trouble-free as in troublesome periods of foster care; in this sense "routine" visits are never uneventful. They may be concerned with the expression of interest in the foster parents as people as well as with recognition of their positive achievement as foster parents. They should help foster parents at the early signs of difficulty to express the negative feelings they may have. It is natural to feel some alarm at the first signs of incipient trouble, but if the foster parents are encouraged to feel their negative feelings of failure and alarm are both natural and allowable, the crisis may be averted.

There is no satisfactory and succinct description of work with foster parents. It is like educational supervision, but only in that it is a limited relationship involving the feelings of both parties concerned; the goals of work with foster parents are not invariably or generally educational. It is work in which casework skills and principles are used to carry out statutory responsibilities on behalf of children. Perhaps the most important casework principle to be recognized in this work is never to treat a person (child or adult) simply as a means. Belief in this principle will beneficially affect the attitude of the worker to natural and foster parents and to children; its application will assist child care officers to value the relationships they establish with parents and children. These relationships are of the essence of child care work. It would be interesting to test the hypothesis that foster home breakdown, about which considerable concern is frequently expressed, is basically connected with "breakdown" in the relationship between worker and foster parent.

So far we have described a general approach illustrated by short extracts; but work with adult or child is more than a series of isolated episodes, even when these are handled with understanding. Something of the difficulties and complexities of foster home supervision over a period of time can be seen in the following record of the placements of Gerald.

The Beginning of Foster Care

Gerald (born 14.7.48) was received into care with his brother George (born 3.5.49) in 1949. Both children were illegitimate and abandoned. He is boarded out in January, 1956, with Mr. and Mrs. Evan, both aged 43, who have two children of their own, Patricia (16) and Edward (9). Mrs. Evan does home dressmaking.

In several respects this is not an ideal placement. Gerald had a short term of psychiatric treatment in 1955 because of his stammer and his aggressive behaviour to other children in the small group home. The psychiatrist recommended that he should be boarded-out in a home where he could be, for a time at least, the only child. This is clearly not the case in the Evan home. However, the ideal in child care is rarely achieved and Gerald was not an easy child to foster; nearly everyone found him not easily likeable. The Evans were of the same religion as Gerald and had successfully reared their own children. They were, moreover, prepared to take Gerald and George and this was considered to have some advantages.

However, fairly soon after the children had been placed Mrs. Evan wrote to the child care officer:

16.1.56. "I have tried to do my best by the children, but I don't think I can make the continual effort. I think you should come and take both children, since it would not be fair to keep one and send the other back to the Children's Home. You should come and take both children at once. The fact of trying to absorb two children into your family with one of your own the same age requires a great deal of mental effort as well as physical. The thing is I don't feel able to keep up the effort being made at the present. To keep one and send back the other I don't feel would be good, now that they have been together here."

20.1.56. Home visit. Mrs. Evan had been in despair but was now not so dismayed, because Gerald was showing some improvement. The child care officer arranged to call in a week's time but (23.1.56) 'phone call from Mrs. Evan requesting the removal of the children. The following day a letter confirmed the 'phone call, stating "The job is beyond me and I hope you will believe I've done my best". A visit is made and George is removed, Mrs. Evan agreeing to keep Gerald.

31.1.56. Letter from Mrs. Evan: "I don't feel happy about keeping Gerald. He is stealing now after George's leaving. I hope you will be able to offer me some advice or a solution. The sad part is I find he has been physically punished for the same thing in . . . (his previous Home), so I don't feel it's any good smacking him . . . What I feel is the hopelessness of combating it all. The situation reminds one of throwing a child in a pond who can't swim and hoping they won't drown."

February and March. A number of home visits are made. Gerald makes some progress. His speech becomes more natural and his physical health improves; he appears more spontaneous and less apathetic. Stealing, however, persists. Mrs. Evan is worried, because she feels she cannot impress on him the serious consequences that would follow. The child care officer tried to reassure Mrs. Evan that this stealing was a symptom of Gerald's insecurity and would clear up when he had been with them for a longer period. The headmaster had congratulated her on her successful coaching of Gerald.

14.4.56. 'Phone call from Mrs. Evan requesting removal. Gerald's stealing persists and Mrs. Evan was particularly worried by his steady lying about it.

Home visit. Mrs. Evan says she can never be sure Gerald is telling the truth. She and her husband both feel they have failed and can make no impression on him. She had "thrashed" Gerald after the last incident (actually spanked him on the legs), but this had produced no improvement at all. The child care officer talked to both foster parents after she had seen Gerald. They both agreed with her that corporal punishment was probably not the best way of coping with Gerald's stealing. She told Mrs. Evan that in her opinion it would be better if she refrained from removing temptation from Gerald's way, as he must be guided to overcome the stealing and not bypass it. She said she felt that they would eventually succeed with Gerald, if all the family were prepared to persevere with him for at least another 10 months. It was highly likely Gerald would steal and lie for some time yet, until he really felt secure. They both asked if there was anything concrete they could do that would help them if they continued their efforts with Gerald, and could they take any line of action after an episode of stealing that would help to cure him. The worker pointed out he was absorbing their values every moment of the day, and their consistent affection and encouragement during the weeks or days when there have been no episodes of stealing constitute a time when he is learning to overcome his defects. She suggested that they should respect Gerald's private property in a marked manner, as this example is likely to convince him more than demonstration of wrath. They both decided to keep Gerald.

16.5.56. Home visit. Mrs. Evan still very disturbed about Gerald. Still stealing both at home and at school. She seemed to be worrying less, but found his lack of penitence and persistent lying difficult to accept. She always takes him to bed every night and stays with him until he settles down to sleep. Gerald saw a play on T.V. recently about a father who lost his child at an early age. He questioned Mrs. Evan very plaintively about this lost baby, and asked if there was any possibility of her having lost him in a similar accident. She was quite distressed by his appeal and said she might have done, and it was wonderful in view of this that he was now living with her . . . Gerald is jealous of Edward as he wants to win the whole of Mrs. Evan's attention. She said Edward had recently been a little insecure himself, because of her attention to Gerald . . . The worker suggested that she tried to let Edward help her with Gerald in the role of an elder brother rather than stressing his equality . . . The child care officer waited until Gerald came home, as usual he came up and informed her that the town she came from was no good.

Comment 1

Now that Gerald has been in his foster home for a few months it is possible to see a certain pattern of behaviour emerging in the foster mother and in the attempts to help her. Mrs. Evan comments on several occasions that she is doing her best, and is clearly worried by problems of adequacy, but there is no record of any attempt to recognize how inadequate (and guilty) she must feel, for example, at the removal of George. Periodically the task of caring for Gerald appears completely hopeless and she can only express her need for help with this despair by demanding Gerald's removal, though it is clear that this demand is not sustained. Her own feelings of hopelessness are not recognized and instead the worker concentrates exclusively on her worry about particular symptoms, *e.g.*, stealing. This leads the foster parents to look for specific instructions and advice, which are extremely difficult to give. In fact the worker relies almost exclusively on reassurance and this amounts to a virtual denial of the problem. When Mrs. Evan talks of "throwing a child in a pond who cannot swim and hoping they won't drown", it is quite probable that she is in fact speaking of herself in relation to the officer. She should be given some support in this situation, but this could have been given more usefully in the form of recognition of her feelings than of specific advice.

The other obvious factor that is beginning to emerge is that Mrs. Evan is investing an important part of herself in this child. She has denied, for example, that he is her foster child. This has important implications for Gerald. The identity of his real parents is a problem for him as well as for Mrs. Evan and the child care officer should certainly have discussed his problem with the foster mother and possibly directly with Gerald himself. On the other hand, Gerald has shown some improvement. Perhaps for the first time he has met someone who may be able, with help, to persevere in maintaining a positive relationship towards him. It is clear that he views the worker's visits as a threat to his growing sense of security. We are faced in this case as in so many with a situation that contains positive and negative factors. Instead, however, of trying to balance these against one another and so reach a decision to continue or terminate the placement we should try to understand what Mrs. Evan is asking of the officer and of Gerald. We should also try to see the patterns of behaviour that Gerald may be showing. One of the important principles in understanding foster home situations is to grasp the ways in which the child characteristically reacts to people and the basis of such reaction in early life. What is it, in other words, in Gerald that has led to the series of problems in his relationship with others?

Help from Other Sources

Visits continue and on

16.7.56. Gerald is taken to a Children's Home for a week's holiday on Mrs. Evan's request.

12.9.56. 'Phone call from Mrs. Evan. Gerald used a brick to hit another boy at school. She feels unable to decide what action to take.

Home visit. Mrs. Evan feels this is the last straw. She has withdrawn Gerald from school pending the advice of the Children's Department. The worker says that they will try to get Gerald to a school for maladjusted children.

18.9.56. School visit. Gerald is to return to school until a place at a maladjusted school is found.

27.9.56. Home visit to reassure Mrs. Evan that the Department was trying to find a place for Gerald. Gerald had been behaving quite well and Mrs. Evan did not wish to part with him if there was any chance of his losing some of his undesirable characteristics. She said she did not find him a nuisance at home. He is fond of her and quite good when he is with her, but is still very jealous of Edward. Mrs. Evan tried to prepare Gerald for removal to another placement, but she feels that she would be acting selfishly if she did not keep him. She wondered if Gerald could be left with her until Christmas, to see if he made any great progress. There is some discussion between the child care officer and Mrs. Evan, and she eventually says she will leave the matter in the officer's hands. If the officer thinks it is advisable she will carry on with Gerald, but if she feels removal is necessary the foster mother will accept her decision. The child care officer apparently agrees to Gerald remaining, and suggests the possibility of some Child Guidance treatment for him.

11.10.56. Child care officer 'phones Mrs. Evan, who is satisfied with Gerald's progress.

9.11.56. 'Phone call from Mrs. Evan requesting a home visit.

Home visit. Mrs. Evan is feeling the continued strain of Gerald on her family and is conscious of a conflict in loyalty. Gerald's latest escapade was to come home and tell her and the local clergyman, who was visiting, that he had hit another boy and been beaten by the headmaster, who had told him he would not be long at that school anyway. Mrs. Evan had contacted the school and discovered that the whole story was a fabrication. The child care officer suggested that when Gerald talked about not being long at school, it might have been a way of seeking reassurance that he would not be sent away from the foster home. Mrs. Evan, however, claimed that he has no deep roots or ties of affection with her or her family, and that leaving them would not create a great problem for him. She finally asked that Gerald be removed within the next two weeks. The worker explained this was a slow process, and asked if Mrs. Evan would be prepared to keep him until a place could be found and an easier transition made. She was unwilling to do this as, she said, the same thing had been said several times before and no action was taken to remove Gerald. The worker had the impression that one of her main complaints was that no one had been to see her to discuss him for several weeks, and she felt she was being left to bear the brunt of his behaviour problems.

10.11.56. Letter from Mrs. Evan that she would keep Gerald until a school could be found for him.

2.1.57. Arrangements made for Gerald to go to a Child Guidance Clinic. After this he is particularly demanding, as he is suspicious of the object of the visit and apprehensive that this might mean removal. He refused to have a meal in X (where the Clinic and Children's Departments are situated) and was anxious to get out of it as soon as possible. Mrs. Evan does feel he is making progress, and seems finally to have accepted the fact that he is deeply attached to her and that a move would disturb him greatly. At the Clinic he was found to be emotionally insecure and it was recommended that he should remain with his foster parents. He is ascertained as maladjusted.

Some progress is made until

1.5.57. A home visit is made in response to a 'phone call from Mrs. Evan, asking for his removal as she can no longer trust him. However, when the worker arrives Mrs. Evan has changed her mind. To request his removal, she says, would be to fail him. She had in fact told him he might be going back to X for a time and the look on his face, a hard, set look, had made her change her mind.

The pattern of 'phone calls requesting removal and a change of mind almost immediately after is repeated twice or three times.

12.11.57. Home visit after Mrs. Evan had written to complain of Gerald's behaviour. The worker explained that everyone sympathized and appreciated the terrific task she had undertaken in caring for Gerald, but that she should face the problem and decide whether she should continue or not. She advised her to consider the effect Gerald was having on her own health and family. She said she would prefer him to go away to school and return there for holidays. She mentioned that both her doctor and the clergyman had impressed her with the damage she would do to Gerald if she rejected him. The worker left her to think it over although Mrs. Evan assured her she wanted to keep him.

In the following year an attempt is again made to obtain some Child Guidance treatment for Gerald.

20.3.58. The child care officer promised Mrs. Evan that she will arrange an appointment at the Clinic so that progress can be assessed.

21.4.58. Mrs. Evan takes Gerald to the Clinic in X. The psychiatrist is still in favour of his staying with Mrs. Evan, but thinks therapy should be arranged.

22.5.58. Weekly treatment sessions begin.

21.7.58. Report from psychiatrist suggests that the foster home is not very satisfactory. Mrs. Evan does not have much understanding of the deeper causes of Gerald's maladjustment, and constantly nags and criticizes him and compares him unfavourably with her own son. The psychiatrist is of the opinion that Gerald would do better in a small family group home where he would be one of a few and not the odd one out.

28.8.58. The child care officer visits the psychiatrist at her own request. She explains that Gerald has already been in a small family group home. The psychiatrist is very concerned about Mrs. Evan's two-way feeling of acceptance and rejection and her exclusive concern with her own worries. The child care officer says she is sure Gerald has first place in the family. In fact Mrs. Evan had sent Edward to go to the psychiatrist with the child care officer so that the psychiatrist could see what Gerald was up against. The psychiatrist will not be offering further appointments. Later that day the child care officer visits Mrs. Evan, who is hostile to the psychiatrist, but the worker cannot discover what actually happened at the Clinic.

Comment 2

It has become increasingly obvious that Mrs. Evan's frequent calls for the removal of Gerald are requests for help for herself. The exact nature of her problem is not so clear, but she is acting out a problem in her persistent rejection and re-acceptance of Gerald. There is some indication that in acting out rejection of Gerald she receives confirmation that she is loved by him (9.11.56; 1.5.57), and that her work is highly valued by the Department and appreciated by the worker. Clearly the relationship with the worker has importance for Mrs. Evan herself—she resented a long interval without visiting (9.11.56)—and her letters and 'phone calls clamour for attention. (In a letter to the worker in November 1958 she says: "You know, Miss Brown, I am really sorry to be a source of worry to you. If all foster parents were such a nuisance you would have no time for the children." It may well be that Mrs. Evan is unconsciously in competition with Gerald for the child care officer, and that she is saying to the worker "I want you to have no time for the children".) This poses a real problem to the officer. How far can she help this foster mother *as* a foster mother without accepting her as a client for casework help in her own right?

The answer to this question depends on a number of factors. How much is Gerald affected by the constant threat to his security? The threat must impinge upon him, but he also shows an affection for Mrs. Evan which he has shown to no one else. What does the ambi-valence in Mrs. Evan mean? What are the forces that divide her?

9

Is it love for Gerald, and then guilt that she does not love her family? It is difficult to answer these questions, because the child care worker has not helped Mrs. Evan to look at the "dark" side of her feelings or even acknowledged that such feelings might exist. It is questionable how far Mrs. Evan should have been allowed to act out her conflict for so long. An attempt is made (12.11.57) to help Mrs. Evan face a realistic view of the conflict but the decision is left too exclusively in her hands. She is clearly incapable of making the decision about keeping Gerald or sending him away. In many ways this seems to be a case in which fostering has been used as a form of treatment for a disturbed child and foster homes are not the equivalents of specialized treatment agencies.

It is unquestionably a complex case, and attempts were made to obtain help for Gerald from the local Child Guidance services. On the whole, these do not seem to have helped anyone very much, officer, foster parent or child. These contacts were discussed with the foster mother in a helpful way, but it is clear that during the last recorded contacts confusion resulted. The confusion could perhaps have been cleared had not the defensiveness of the psychiatrist and the feelings of the child care worker interfered so that this communication was imperfect.

Placement in the Maladjusted School

December, 1959. Mrs. Evan takes Gerald to see the Maladjusted School. She feels she has failed with him.

28.12.59. Home visit. The worker told Mrs. Evan the final arrangements about Gerald and the school. The whole visit was very emotional. Gerald was worried about the school. He could not visualize a boarding-school and kept thinking in terms of a Children's Home. Mrs. Evan was overwrought, wondering if she had let him down. Gerald was most meticulous in placing the school, relating it to a large town nearby. The worker discovered he had visited with Mrs. Evan and Edward a friend of Mrs. Evan who was in a mental hospital. He had a secret fear that he was going there. She instanced all the T.V. programmes where boys' boarding-schools figured, to try and convince him that a school was completely unlike a Home, and that it was a school not a Home he was going to. What made most difference was the fact that by going to the school he was losing 2 days' holiday. He considered all schools went back on the same day . . .

5.1.60. Escorted Gerald and Mrs. Evan to the school. It was a very emotional journey. Mrs. Evan did not keep her tears back and Gerald became paler. He played up, demanding tit-bits. When we arrived he became really worried. The Head was reassuring, but Gerald clung to Mrs. Evan.

Comment 3

A place in a maladjusted school is ultimately found and Mrs. Evan agrees to have Gerald home for holidays. This seems a helpful way of dealing with the problem, since, whatever Mrs. Evan's own emotional problems, she has provided Gerald with some stability and has been the only person who has persevered with him. The child care officer encourages Mrs. Evan to participate actively in the arrangements for Gerald's placement, and this is helpful to both foster parent and child. It recognizes Mrs. Evan's place in the life of the child, and shows Gerald that this is a plan for which Mrs. Evan has some positive feeling. In addition to this the child care officer herself helps Gerald to realize something of what the school will be like.

CHAPTER 7

WORKING WITH FAMILIES

IN an important sense most of the work of child care involves working, directly or indirectly, with families. When we take a child from his natural family we try to provide a substitute family. The child, of course, even though he is physically separated from his parents, carries them within him, so that they and his feelings about them are an important feature of his present situation. In this chapter, however, some of the special ways in which child care officers work directly with natural families will be considered. These may be seen as:

(i) Help to families to part with their children and, perhaps, to share their care permanently with others;

(ii) help to families to regain care of their children;

(iii) help to families to retain this care.

The general principle of all such work could be very briefly summarized as follows: these people are parents, but they are not only parents.

(i) **Helping Families to Part with their Children**

In a busy professional life, when so many demands are made upon the existing staff, it is easy to neglect the valuable work that might be done with parents at the time of separation. This is especially true when children are removed by court order. It is at this moment that the child can begin to "die" in his parents' feelings and, for the sake of both parent and child, the child care worker should do what she can to keep the child "alive". This is primarily a question of the way in which she carries out the functions she has in any case to perform. It may be that she has to gather information about the child's past history, so that a decision can be reached about placement, or explanations have to be made about visiting.

In each of these contacts it is useful to consider the likely feelings of the parents, and the way the worker explains the reality of the situation to them.

If a child has been removed from the care of the parents, it is likely that they will feel guilty at the public condemnation of their bad parenthood and that they will mourn the loss of their children. It is, however, unlikely that the worker will see such feelings openly displayed. She may instead meet anger, apparent lack of concern, or intense hostility against herself. The parents may in fact be already beginning to withdraw from their role of parents, which has presented them with so much pain. Faced with cases of severe neglect, it is easy for workers to feel punitive towards the neglectful parents, and to forget that these parents have pain, unhappiness and needs of their own. These needs may often be asserted, often at a childish level. Thus, insistence on the value of visiting from the child's point of view sufficiently recognizes neither their own negative feelings towards their children, nor their own demands for attention and nurture. Recognition of the parents as parents can sometimes be given by seeking their co-operation in the attempt to build a social history of the child, as well as to help in planning for the future, but this must be felt by the parents as recognition, not an insistent pressure to be "good".

Take, for example, the case of Paula (born in 1940) and taken into care in November, 1950. She is illegitimate and there is no regular cohabitee. Early in January, 1951, the Children's Officer writes to the mother that she "would welcome the opportunity to discuss Paula with her in order to make the best provision for her future, and could see the mother almost any day next week by appointment". This contains the implicit assumption that this mother is concerned for her child's future; but with parents whose children have to be removed it is often important to go out and visit them even though there might have been much activity on the officer's part before the actual court hearing. This shows the parent the worker continues to be interested, and also recognizes that such parents may need more active encouragement to participate than an open invitation to call at the office. Elkan, after three years' work in a Children's Reception Centre, stated that she had found that

"where parents have been left to themselves after their children's removal, or where attempts to approach them have failed, they have frequently neither visited nor written, and have behaved as if the child no longer existed."[1]

The maintenance of some contact between parent and child is not merely a recognition of the value of parents, even neglectful ones. It is also a helpful measure from the point of view of the child. In some cases contact with real parents or even the apparent reminder of their existence must be painful, and child care officers who have to witness such pain must often wonder if it serves any purpose. It serves in fact several purposes in the life of the child. It can help him to face the reality of his situation. He may well imagine that separation from his home has been caused by his own badness—no-one could stand him any longer. He may imagine that his parents are dead. In either case he begins unconsciously to feel guilt. This may result in some kind of idealization of the parents, so that the negative feeling which is commonly combined with the positive in any significant relationship is "split off" and may come to dominate his present relationship, for example with foster parents. Briefly, the maintenance of some contact helps the child to face the reality of separation, and may lessen his sense of worthlessness and the necessity to take refuge in fantasy.

There are, of course, administrative measures which are sometimes believed to help maintain the interest of the parents in their children. Under s. 10 of the Children Act, 1948, where children who are under the age of 16 are received into care under s. 1, the parents "shall secure that the appropriate local authority are informed of the parent's address for the time being". Under s. 23 they are obliged to make contributions toward the cost of the child in care. It is sometimes suggested that this helps parents to retain some sense of responsibility towards their children, and the collection of such contributions is sometimes made part of the work of the child care officer. This is a matter of some difference of opinion within the Service. Some officers believe that persistent concern for contributions and assessment interferes with any relationship they may be forming with the parents. The opposing argument may be stated in the words of a well-known report of a Children's Department:

"It should be borne in mind that when visiting, the visitor covers the whole of the relationship between the family and the Children's

[1] Elkan, I., "Interviews with Neglectful Parents", *British Journal of Psychiatric Social Work*, 1956, Vol. III, No. 3.

Department, and whilst dealing with the possibilities of the child's return home, also takes up the matter of contributions to the cost of the child in care. Thus, whilst encouraging the parents' own efforts to provide accommodation, a worker may be informed that the husband and wife are both working, and consequently their contributions can be re-assessed on their higher income. Very often such an increased assessment may be an added incentive to the parents in their efforts to find a suitable place to live."[1]

It is an important argument of this book that the casework relationship in child care is not something that can be considered apart from objectives derived from the letter and spirit of statutory and administrative regulation. The casework relationship is not cultivated for its own sake. However, the concept of agency function does not bind the caseworker to accept every administrative means to the achievement of the purposes of the agency. Parental contributions have to be collected by the Children's Department, but there is room for legitimate difference of opinion on which personnel in the Department should be responsible for this part of the work. Casework principle and experience perhaps help us to decide. We need to judge this issue by considering the characteristics of the people from whom the caseworker may have to attempt to extract contributions. Very often they are people who can feel little but their own needs in the situation. They find it difficult to conceive the possible function of the social worker except as a punitive force in their lives, or as a potential threat, perhaps of the removal of their other children or of the possibility that they may have to face unpleasant facts about their own feelings and behaviour. It is argued here not that such parents are to be shielded forever from such facts, but that in order to help the needful parents we should ensure that there is an initial focus which they can accept. The most important task with neglectful parents is to begin to help them towards involvement in the solution of their own problems, and to do this it must very often prove a distraction for the same officer to be concerned with them as people and as parents capable of immediate acceptance of the financial burden of children from whom they have been separated. In many cases it would seem, therefore, helpful to divide the collection of contributions from the main rehabilitative approach to such clients. But where such a division of responsibility is undertaken, or even where it is judged that no

[1] *The First Four Years* (cited at p. 22, *ante*), p. 24.

rehabilitation is possible, contributions should always be collected or pursued with regard to the feelings of the parents and to the symbolic value of what they offer or refuse. For administrative staff to adopt such an approach, it may be useful for Children's Departments to consider some form of in-training along the lines of the seminars in human relations recently started for National Assistance Board officials.

To suggest that the regular collection of contributions from certain kinds of people may prove a hindrance to the work of rehabilitation is not to suppose that the child care worker never deals with money. Take, for example, the case of Judy Brown:

> Judy Brown (16) has been taken into care by another authority, and her home authority is asked to contact Mrs. Brown about Judy's clothes and her outstanding clothing cheque for £5. How much of this would Mrs. Brown be able to pay? The worker calls on Mrs. Brown, and finds her very non-committal about her daughter, who has run away from home. The worker seeks to elicit some history, and discovers that Mr. Brown, a younger man than his wife, is Mrs. Brown's second husband. Mrs. Brown is very reluctant to pay anything towards the clothing cheque, but expands very little on what the worker senses is strong negative feeling against her daughter. Two or three visits are made in connection with this matter and the mother, encouraged by the worker, states that she has suspicions about her husband's relationship with Judy. She had confronted him with it, but he had denied anything improper, in spite of Judy's suggestive behaviour. Mrs. Brown asks the worker to keep this information confidential, but expresses some relief that she has been able to talk to someone about it.

In this extract the worker called about a financial matter, but she sensed from what Mrs. Brown said that her attitude to Judy's clothing cheque was not simply reluctance to contribute. It was an aspect of her feelings towards Judy. In this case the mother is able to move from a discussion of finance to other matters, but in the case of the neglectful or problem family it is often difficult to "move" in a relationship that has been established on one basis (finance) to another. In the Brown case, too, the financial issue does not seem overwhelmingly provocative to the client.

We have so far discussed helping parents to part with their children and the question of maintaining contact between child and parent. In some instances, however, our work should be aimed at helping child and parent to remain apart. The case of Jennifer A. in Chapter 4 is an illustration of a situation in which this may well be the aim. Parents of children taken into care under s. 1 of the

Children Act, 1948, may well appear time and time again to claim the children and yet, because of their disturbed personalities, they are incapable of giving them consistent treatment and basic security. These parents are, in fact, acting out their own difficulties in a parental relationship by continually and angrily separating from their children and then happily uniting and re-uniting with them.

Take, for example, the case of Daniel Jones (8), the illegitimate son of a woman now married to Mr. George, by whom she has two girls, four years and one year. Daniel had been placed by his mother in several private foster homes, whilst she moved around the country taking jobs for two or three weeks at a time, but continually writing to Daniel and his various foster mothers that she planned to be reunited with him within a few days. Sometimes she would visit the foster home and remove Daniel with little or no warning. In the last private home, where Daniel had been fostered for a year, and from which he was later taken into care, Mrs. George would visit spasmodically, taking Daniel to her new home for a few days. She said she was not able to have him at home permanently because of her husband, but each time Daniel was returned to his foster home he was dirty and unkempt and seemed to be withdrawn.

After Daniel came into care, Mrs. George was visited by the child care officer, who wanted to assess the possibilities of rehabilitation. The Georges were living in an old terraced house spotlessly clean and tidy; the two girls were very clean, and had dresses made of the same material as their mother's. Mr. George was at home, though the appointment had been made specifically to see his wife. He played with the children during the interview, and spoke of his desire to make a home for Daniel. Mrs. George intervened to say that there wasn't room for them all. The worker enquired about sleeping accommodation and Mrs. George said there were three bedrooms, but she used one for storage and dressmaking (she took in work of various kinds). The worker wondered if she had to do this work. Mr. George looked ill at ease but said nothing. Mrs. George said that she didn't *have* to, but it meant she could buy extra things for herself and could ensure that the children look very nice—"not like some round here". The worker asked what Mrs. George thought was the best way to plan for Daniel's future. "Well", she said, "I didn't want him in a Home, people would talk and besides . . ." "Besides what?" asked the worker. "Well, I've been in a Home myself and I know."

The worker took this opportunity to obtain some of Mrs. George's history. Her mother owned a small business and was an elected local authority member. Her father was a waster, who was away for long periods, but would return home from time to time with wonderful presents. "You always knew when he was home, there were wrappings from presents everywhere, and the house would get more and more untidy and mother angrier and angrier." Mrs. George seemed to be her father's favourite. Then one night there was a quarrel and her father struck her mother. The mother became very ill and the father went away, leaving Mrs. George to look after the home. "I never saw or spoke of him from that day on." Later Mrs. George had to be admitted to a Children's Home, and soon afterwards, her mother died.

The worker was encouraged by her rapport with Mrs. George as suggested by the unfolding of this story. Mr. George had made an excuse to leave soon after his wife began to tell her story. The worker ended the interview by saying that since Mrs. George had experienced institutional life away from her parents she would know what this was like, and did she want it for Daniel? The worker would call again to talk this over.

The following day Mrs. George 'phoned. She would like Daniel home next week. Could the worker arrange this? She had decided to give up her dressmaking. The worker said she would call and discuss this. However, it seemed that mother would not be at home any time in the next two weeks.

In this case it would seem that Daniel has become the target for some of the feelings originally connected with his grandfather. By leaving Daniel and then uniting with him Mrs. George creates in someone else the feelings of desertion and of reunion she experienced as a child. Yet the course of her ambivalent feeling in this original situation was halted when her father made her mother ill, and Mrs. George split her feelings so that her father became completely bad and unmentionable, and she identified herself strongly with the controlled, tidy, mother. The situation is, of course, probably much more complicated than this, but even a superficial view suggests that this may well be a case in which the aim of work with Mrs. George is to help her to keep separated from her son. It should not be assumed that because she can apparently look after her girl children she can offer consistent care to the boy. The way she responds to the officer, with a detailed story of her life, suggests a possibility that Mrs. George is capable of taking help, but this apparently hopeful sign must be further tested. Lack of reticence and reserve is sometimes an indication of problematic personality structure; an inability, as it were, to retain anything.

The aim of work may well be to help Mrs. George not to act out her ambivalence towards this boy as directly as she used in the past, and to help her as a mother to co-operate in a plan to secure his best interests. It may be possible to achieve this by helping Mrs. George to see something of what she seems to be doing in the situation. It would be useful, for example, to encourage her to express some of her anger at her father. It might then be possible to turn her attention to the way in which she displaces some of the feeling originally aroused by him on to her son. The officer might comment that it is strange that mother cannot make up her mind about Daniel—he is her son and she does not want him to go into a Home, but something makes her treat him in a different way, almost as if he reminded her of his grandfather. Such an approach would help the worker to see if Mrs. George could use and develop insight into the problem. It indicates fairly clearly what the worker sees in the situation, but the suggestions are made in a supportive and tentative way, not as criticisms.

This kind of mother is frequently known as a "rejecting" mother. This term is deceptively simple; it can be useful in child care work merely as indication of the general area in which a search for explanation can begin. Newell in two quite early studies[1] drew attention to several factors directly related to rejection; loss of social life because of childbirth, fear that the child had inherited bad tendencies, disgust or fear concerning pregnancy, and forced marriage. He found in a study of 33 unwanted children that rejection was indirectly connected with unhappy marital adjustment, and in a second study of 75 children that the connection was direct. He found, too, that rejection could be expressed not only by cruelty and neglect but also by overprotection and by inconsistent handling. Incidentally, half of these children felt their mothers lacked affection for them and much of their difficult behaviour seemed to be the result of their own discovery and acting out of what their mothers feared most. These two studies suggest, then, that maternal rejection can take a number of different forms and be connected with a number of factors. Anna Freud[2] has also drawn attention to the different motivations of rejecting mothers. What is required, therefore, is not to use the label "rejecting mother" as a helpful diagnosis, but to search further for what it is she rejects in the child and for what reasons.

(ii) Helping Families to Regain Care of their Children

This is often called work of rehabilitation and, as we have seen, there is an obligation on the Children's Department to attempt to

[1] Newell, H. W., "The Psycho-Dynamics of Maternal Rejection", *American Journal of Orthopsychiatry*, Vol. 4, pp. 387–401, 1934. Also, "A Further Study of Maternal Rejection", Vol. 6, pp. 576–589, 1936.

[2] Freud, A., "Safeguarding the Emotional Health of our Children", Casework Papers, Family Service Association of America, 1954.

secure that children admitted under s. 1 of the Act of 1948 are returned to parents and relatives "where it appears to them (the local authority) consistent with the welfare of the child". An increasing amount of rehabilitative work is also undertaken with children committed to the local authority by the court under s. 5. It is quite common practice to return children to their homes while the court order still applies.

Much of what follows in section (iii) applies to helping families regain care of their children and material already discussed in section (i) is relevant. In this section I wish only to discuss one important matter, the grounds on which a decision is reached that it is consistent with the welfare of the child that he be returned home. This is a difficult decision, but even though the court makes the initial decision to remove the child under section 5, the professional staff must reach a decision in the light of their judgment on the situation as they see it. The following case illustrates some of the difficulty from the point of view of working with the parents. It is not a recent case and may not reflect general practice, but the lesson it teaches is important:

> Philip (9) was committed to care because of neglect in January, 1951, under a Fit Person Order. After the court hearing, the child care officer talked to his mother and the man with whom she was cohabiting. She heard about their circumstances and stressed how important Philip's mother was to the boy. The worker impressed on the couple the importance of securing permanent and suitable accommodation.
>
> In the course of 1951 the couple moved several times, but Philip was not allowed home for Christmas because of the unsuitable accommodation. In 1952 permanent accommodation was found and the mother applied to the juvenile court for a revocation of the order. In court the department stated that Philip appeared to have settled well in care and the magistrates rejected the application.

In this brief extract the "parents" were led to believe that the provision of a good material environment was crucial, and that securing permanent accommodation would be of the greatest use to their case for the revocation of the order. The worker may have emphasized the material difficulties because she felt that this was the only difficulty that the "parents" could admit. However, the record does not indicate that any attempt was made to involve them in a discussion of their feelings in connection with Philip or how they in fact saw themselves as parents. It is undoubtedly difficult to help parents when the Department has had some part to play in the removal of the child, but to discuss with them only one aspect of the case may result in the parents feeling, at least, misunderstood, and, at most, betrayed when they meet in court the situation which faced Philip's "parents".

In planning the return home the general principle formulated at the beginning of this chapter can be usefully applied. It is easy in such cases to stress the parental roles to the exclusion of others, and to adopt an unhelpful judge-like attitude. This is, of course, to suggest not that the behaviour of many parents can be condoned, but that the worker stands more chance of helping the parents to change if her attitude is one of understanding rather than moralizing. Take, for example, the following extract from the case of a mother who has moved around the country a great deal, but who visited her children in care fairly consistently:

> 10.3.59. Mrs. Brooks came as arranged and we told her that as soon as possible the children would be moving here, but it was impressed on Mrs. Brooks that she must now settle here, as it was very bad for the children to keep having these changes. She said that Mr. Brooks had still not turned up and the worker asked her who she would put first if he did, the children or Mr. Brooks, and she assured her that she had realized finally that her children must come first, as Mr. Brooks was not interested in them at all, and in any case he was not Barry's father. She is still fond of Mr. Brooks and admits this, and it is not easy to judge whether she would really put the children first, but she says she is missing them very much and will be very glad when they come here. As far as can be gathered, therefore, from her, she has every intention of putting the children first.

Here the mother is called on to make a choice that appears in some ways unreal and unnecessary. The emphasis placed on this decision by the worker cannot help the mother to explore her predicament or to feel confident that her problem is understood. It seems that we sometimes make the question of return home dependent on "good" behaviour, rather than trying to base it on decisions reached by child care officer and parent after considered investigation. In the following extract it is the good behaviour of the child that is apparently regarded as crucial:

> 8.11.58. I brought Margaret (8) from her foster home to meet her mother; she was very talkative on the way, and told me all about her school and what she did where she lived. When we arrived at the office her mother had not yet come, so I asked Margaret if she wished to return to her mother for good, and she said that she did. I then told her that I wanted her to behave this weekend, and I wanted to

hear from her mother and foster mother that she had been a good girl,
and then I was going to think about her going back to her mother to
live. She promised that she would be good as she very much wanted
this. When her mother came I repeated this to Mrs. Worth, and said
I should be asking if Margaret had been good or not when I collected
her on Sunday. Mrs. Worth took Margaret off for a walk around the
market.

What should be seen as crucial is neither good behaviour nor
improved material standards, but the attempt to see how relationships within the family have changed and to assess the way in
which the family functions in the present and in particular how it
deals with stress.

(iii) Helping Families to Retain Care of their Children

This work is often called "preventive" work. The notion of
"prevention" is not unambiguous. It can apply to measures that
ensure that a Children's Department does not take responsibility
for a particular child, by arranging with more or less imagination
and varying degrees of conscientiousness, some alternative course of
action. It can refer to maintaining a situation and forestalling
deterioration, or to ensuring that the need for social service does not
arise because the conditions underlying the problems are not
created. Each of these is a worthy objective, but it is essential to
be clear about the way in which the term is used. "Prevention" in
the first sense often contradicts prevention in the second sense. For
example, in an article on "Preventive Casework in a Children's
Department", it is observed that "provided the need is established,
the children of families with whom the preventive officer is working
should be received into care for short periods at his request as part
of the preventive effort".[1]

In this section work with neglectful or "problem" families will
alone be discussed, and "prevention" will be used in the sense of
preventing the break-up of the family and the deterioration of
situations already containing problematic features. As even a
superficial acquaintance with the literature on problem families
indicates, the dimensions of their problems must often seem overwhelming. In this chapter we can indicate only some of the
characteristics of the families, and some principles that may help to

[1] Easton, R., "Preventive Work in Children's Departments", *Case Conference*,
February, 1959.

formulate an approach to their manifold problems. It is recognized that the time which can be given to "preventive" work in each Department is limited, sometimes by pressure of other work, sometimes by deliberate policy. Some authorities have appointed workers to specialize in working with such families and others would rather see such work carried out by other agencies, leaving the Children's Departments to develop specialized services for the treatment of the deprived child. Yet all Departments will have contact with such families, and it is important that every agency having short-term or long-term contact with them should consider how their approaches can be made more helpful.

These neglectful or problem families have featured largely in social work and popular literature since the end of the Second World War. Much of the interest has been essentially unproductive, and whilst certain interesting aspects of problem family behaviour have been described and one or two explanatory ideas proposed, there has been no vigorous attempt to establish any theories. We can probably accept as a reasonable idea of the "problem family" the descriptions to be found in Stephens' *Problem Families* (now out of print), though many needful families would not perhaps show all the classical features of dirt, disorder and repeated disaster. Some writers have suggested that "syndromes" of problem family behaviour have been established, but this is not the case. We are still faced with a variety of "symptoms" but no one is quite sure what they are symptoms of.

Yet it is possible to penetrate this variety of behaviour and to organize it around certain key notions, crude though these may be. Briefly we can describe the problems of many neglectful families in the following statements: (a) these families present problems in the management of daily life of a serious and repetitive kind, (b) these problems can often be seen as problems in relationships between family members and between the family and the outside world; (c) these families have considerable difficulty in using help to work on their problems.

(a) In America, Wiltse[1] has suggested that it is events that govern these families rather than they who govern events, and it does seem that their lives follow a round of crises. What seems simple to some

[1] Wiltse, K. T., "The Hopeless Family", *Social Work* (U.S.A.), Vol. 3, No. 4, October, 1958.

people (*e.g.* a visit to a doctor because of some unexplained discomfort, an explanation to a teacher about a child's absence) seems to present very great difficulty to the problem family. If we look more closely at such behaviour, however, we will see that it has two important aspects. It is due in part to the stress of wrestling against a very demanding environment with meagre resources; and it is also due to the interaction of personality on environment. Even with the small amount of research that has been done on this and related topics, it is clear that these families are among the most vulnerable in our society. They bear many of the marks of potential and often actual poverty. In the first place, they are often large families, and research since the 1930's has accustomed us to the idea that the young family takes a high economic toll of the parents, particularly in a child-centred society. The heads of such families are often in unskilled occupations. Wilson has drawn attention to the impact of economic stress in families with a low-wage earner where income may be substantially below subsistence level.[1] Problem families, too, may often, for a variety of reasons, be alienated from their families of origin, and thus deprived of help in the rearing of a large family. They often live in housing that ranges from the inconvenient to the apparently impossible, and in conditions that make life a struggle.

Such environmental stress, however, cannot be separated (in the context of helping these families) from the personalities of family members concerned. Objective difficulties have their subjective connections. As Woodhouse has suggested,

> "a low standard of material existence may be perceived by some clients as confirming their own worthlessness—they feel they deserve no better, as it were. Others may perceive their situation as an expression of the lack of love and of being given to, that they have always sought but never found."[2]

This view does not imply that such families will not benefit from material help or a changed environment. It indicates that help should be given in a way that makes some contact with these inner feelings.

(*b*) In problem families, relationship difficulties are often seen

[1] Wilson, H., "Problem Families and the Concept of Immaturity", *Case Conference*, October, 1959.
[2] Woodhouse, D. L., "Casework with Problem Families", *Case Conference*, June, 1958.

between parents, or between parents and children. Many babies in such families receive good mothering, but when the controlling element in parent roles has to be exercised uncertain handling often results in wavering between angry rejection (of the child) and sullen acquiescence in his "bad" behaviour. Within the marriage relationship sharing is a common problem. The man may value in his wife only the role of wife (not that of mother), a wife may find it hard to share a man's attention with his friends. The worker may meet all kinds of specific complaints about relationships when working with such a family, but most of them will be concerned basically with questions about the person's capacity to love, and ability to be loved, and with fears about his capacity to destroy and vulnerability in the face of destruction.

One concept that has been given attention in the literature is that of immaturity. This was first propounded by Irvine in 1954[1] and has been since expanded and criticized as one of the central concepts for understanding the problem family. It is now clear that the term is used to refer to both regression under massive stress (secondary immaturity) and arrested emotional development (primary); that it refers to modes of feeling as well as concrete behaviour, and is seen as arising from a lack of crucial relationships at certain stages of early social and emotional development. Criticism of the concept has argued that the term is not explanatory, and that before searching for causes in terms of personality we should look first for stress in the external world.

The concept is, of course, not seen by its proponents as explanatory. Immaturity has to be explained in any particular case, but by using the term we can perhaps bring together in a helpful way symptoms otherwise seen as separate. The term draws attention to the relationships, past and present, of problem family members, and suggests that some of the mechanisms and attitudes seen in early relationships between infants and parents are operative in the lives of these adult parents. Many problem family parents are still working out in a basic way the very early emotional problems of love and hate, and are still undecided about their own inner goodness and the trustworthy nature of the outside world. In these respects the concept has directed our attention to important problems. It

[1] Irvine, E. E., "Research into Problem Families", *British Journal of Psychiatric Social Work*, Spring, 1954.

10

can, however, still be only very generally applied. We cannot, at present at any rate, make a precise statement that this person, for example, behaves at the level of a three-year-old or a two-year-old. Similarly, when we speak of playing a parental role with the families, this is only a very general statement, since we know little in fact of what in detail the "good" parent does for children at different ages. The picture presented by problem families is frequently not simply one of immaturity (in a general sense), but may contain elements of immaturity together with, for example, genuine neurotic problems.

(c) The relationships within problem families are often exacerbated by their relationships with outside bodies of various kinds. These difficulties often derive from their social position, at the bottom of the social scale, where they are frequently treated by other social groups and institutions in ways that lessen their self-esteem. The participation of members of problem families in institutional life (trade unions, schools, etc.) is minimal, and they find it difficult to learn or take creatively from a social system in which they have little or no place. Thus their contacts with social institutions are often passively or aggressively fearful. They may act as if social institutions were created almost to satisfy their own deep needs or as if they expected punitive criticism, but in either case the institution is seen as something essentially apart from themselves, not something in which they could play a co-operating part.

The relationship problems already mentioned indicate a generalized difficulty in maintaining realistic, mutually satisfying contact with another person over any length of time. Thus when a social worker appears to offer such a contact, the reaction is often one of fear. This is partly fear of expected criticism, but also a deeper fear based on doubts about what this relationship may accomplish in them or for them. Relationships may be mistrusted because they have failed so often in the past to satisfy the great needs of these people. The particular relationship may be feared because the client feels a threat to his established ways (conscious and unconscious) of dealing with life.

This brief indication of some of the problems facing neglectful families serves to suggest some broad features of the way help might be offered.

(i) The problems of these families interact so intricately that help needs to be offered to the family as a whole.

(ii) The problems are manifold and extensive, and their solution depends on the co-operation of several services as a minimum requirement.

(iii) Help has to be taken to these families, and offered with persistence and skill on focalized problems.

(i) *The Family as a Whole.*—The notion of help to the family as a whole is not new; the late nineteenth-century caseworker had some familiarity with the concept, but defined it mainly in economic terms. The practical implications of this have been illustrated briefly at the beginning of Chapter 3. Another way of using the concept can be illustrated from probation in the second and third decade of the present century, when there was emphasis upon knowing and making contact with every family member. In contemporary usage "family as a whole" refers to the family regarded as a system of interacting relationships. To offer help to the family as a whole means not that every member and every problem will be approached, but that decisions about which member and which problem to tackle will be based on some appraisal of how the family functions as a unit. At present it is not easy to make such an appraisal, because of deficiencies in knowledge. Knowledge that helps in the appraisal of an individual is not always useful in appraising a small interacting group of individuals. Consequently, attempts have been made in America to use such concepts as "transaction", "interaction", etc., to describe behaviour and feeling that does not result from the conscious or unconscious activity of any one person in the family group. Perhaps of more immediate use is the notion of role and personality "fit" described in this country, for example, by Rapoport and Rosow.[1] This notion seeks to draw attention both to the roles people hold in our society (*e.g.*, father, sister, neighbour), and to the way in which two complementary roles (*e.g.*, husband–wife; mother–father) do or do not "fit" together to produce a system that works reasonably well. The system is judged to work well if it is accomplishing the given tasks of

[1] Rapoport, R., and Rosow, I., "An Approach to Family Relationships and Role Performance", *Human Relations*, 1957, Vol. X, No. 3, 209–221.

the role relationship (*e.g.*, in the case of mother–father, the adequate rearing of children) and also if it satisfies the emotional needs of the partners. In trying to understand the "family as a whole" social workers may find it useful to think of family relationships in terms of the characteristic ways in which family members handle their social roles and how this "fits" with the behaviour and expectation of others. Thus attention can be directed on the one hand to the roles that are accepted, or about which the holder feels conflict, or those that he has not had adequate opportunity to learn, and on the other, to the way in which this acceptance or failure is viewed by himself and by his partner.

Yet it is not only lack of knowledge that prevents social workers using the notion of "family as a whole" to the fullest advantage. There are also more practical aspects to this problem. How frequently do workers ignore, both in their visits and assessments, the presence of the father or some important member of the extended family? Workers often write only to the mother, and their tacit failure to include the father in planning, for example, the future of a child must often have the pathological effect of increasing his withdrawal from family affairs.

The family, then, must be studied and helped "as a whole". This does not mean that child care officers have to undertake a heavy burden of "intensive" casework within families. It does, however, necessitate a particular kind of approach on the part of the child care officer and a rational division of work with other agencies in the framework of an ongoing attempt to see the family "as a whole". In other words, it draws attention to the importance of co-operation between the Children's Department and other social agencies.

(ii) *Co-operation.*—This is a much-used word representing an apparent ideal in social welfare. The reality of practice leaves much to be desired. It is not simply, as Donnison has pointed out,[1] that by co-operation we sometimes mean referral of families to more or less appropriate agencies, and sometimes close and active pursuance of a plan worked out with these other agencies. It is rather a neglect of two important facets of the problem. In seeking and pursuing co-operation (in the second sense) we often neglect the fact that the problems of families (particularly families that raise such anxiety

---

[1] Donnison, D. V., *Child Neglect and the Social Services*, 1954.

and consequent social condemnation as "problem families") frequently, as it were, overflow onto the agencies, involving them in relationship problems with each other. It is often quite easy, for example, for the mother or father of such a family to play off one agency against another, as they used to find safety by playing off their own parents. The second aspect frequently forgotten is the importance of "presenting" the members of these families to other agencies concerned. These are families who expect criticism, if not punishment, from most of the social institutions with which they have contact. They need help if they are to communicate effectively with such institutions. The institutions may also need help.

Take, for example, the following short recording of a school visit:

> The Child Care Officer called to see the Headmistress of X School to obtain information about Tommy (6). The Headmistress says she is afraid there is not much she can say about Tommy. She has been very busy and does not, in any event, have time to devote to problem cases. His mother has called at the school to complain about the way his teacher treated him. The mother seemed mental. The officer wondered how Tommy got on with other children. The headmistress said she would call his teacher.

The amount of time a child spends in school and the effect of school performance and school relationships on his estimate of his own worth indicates the value of school life for him. It is, therefore, important that workers try to bring school and child and family into as meaningful a contact as possible. Child care officers often regard the schools as the source or recipient of simple information, but greater attention to the feelings of school staff will result in more fruitful communication between staff and worker and, perhaps, an improved relationship between school and child. In the extract above, the headmistress seems to feel the visit of the officer as a threat of some kind. She is perhaps angry with Tommy, his mother and the worker—she is *afraid* she cannot say much about Tommy. She may feel that the worker has somehow come to complain as Tommy's mother complained. She may see the situation as hopeless because Tommy's mother is "mental". In the face of these possibilities it would have been better not to press for information but to express some understanding of the headmistress's difficulty, and to give some indication that the worker was looking forward to a discussion of common difficulties rather than expecting detailed and lengthy information. She would certainly have to show some

sympathy with the headmistress over the mother's "attack" before
she tried to arouse sympathy for Tommy or his mother.

(iii) *Help has to be offered with persistence and with specific problems.*—
Help has to be offered to these families in ways which make it
acceptable. These families, on the whole, cannot be expected to
come for regular appointments at an office or to carry out arrangements made for the near future. As previously indicated, offers of
help are not seen as such, at least in the early stages. But what
sort of "help" can be offered by staff of Children's Departments?
Offers of unspecified "help" can be as overwhelmingly useless for
the family as they can be drastically confusing for the worker.

It would seem appropriate for child care officers to accept as the
focus of their work the relationships and problems between children
and parents. We have seen that this can be helpful even for the
child temporarily or permanently separated from his home. It is as
helpful in "preventive" work. This does not mean that the parent
is seen simply and insistently as a parent. He is seen as a person
with his own needs and problems, but the worker sees these problems
in relation to his position as parent. For example, a mother may be
helped to make and carry out plans to improve her own health.
This expresses the worker's genuine concern for her as a person but
also furthers the long-term objective of making it easier for her to
be a parent.

In general, help is often offered in material form. This may meet
an immediate crisis and, as the Pacifist Service Unit workers first
demonstrated, shows concern and a real desire to help, to people
who may, for a variety of reasons, be of limited verbal ability. The
value of such assistance creates a difficulty for Children's Departments, since they are at the moment allowed to spend money only on
children in care. A second difficulty concerns the fears that always
arise of increased dependency if material aid is given. If, as a child
care officer has written, "it is not practical for any agency to work
with problem families unless it is able to provide some material
help",[1] how can Children's Departments meet the two difficulties
involved?

The first difficulty is purely practical, and various funds and
resources of a voluntary kind can be used. It is also likely that new
legislation, following the Ingleby Report, may widen the powers of

[1] Easton, R., *op. cit.*

Children's Departments in this respect. The second difficulty is more serious. Yet there are families that may never be independent in any full sense of the term for any length of time. It would be unrealistic to suppose, as did caseworkers in the C.O.S., that every man was as capable as his neighbour of full economic independence. Caseworkers worry over dependence from time to time, but Waldron[1] in this country has argued recently for the greater "Acceptance of Dependency in Social Casework". Whether caseworkers are "for" or "against" dependency, it is nearly always viewed as some kind of "global" phenomenon—people are or are not dependent. Some of the caseworker's anxiety about dependency may be relieved if she asks in what areas the client seems to be dependent, what is the degree of dependency, and, perhaps more important, what is the client seeking through dependency. In other words, dependency should not be regarded as some kind of basic characteristic of a person. There is every reason to suppose that some kind of dependency exists in all close relationships. The question that should always demand an answer is what does this person seek through this piece of dependent behaviour, from what fear, for example, does he seek protection or what are the internal obstacles to independence?

Material help can be offered to meet a crisis, in a way that makes contact with some of the inner needs of the client. Viewing the matter in this light, material relief is seen as part of a general programme of help designed for a particular family, which will consist largely of behaviour towards the family members encouraging them to feel the worker is to be trusted as she helps them to deal with their concrete problems of living in a way that brings relief for their emotional problems.

Within the focus appropriate to the Children's Department the officer will, then, often offer help over concrete problems of day-to-day care of children. She will also nearly always be concerned with the family's relationship to authority. This may well be one of the impediments to effective co-operation with the family that she will have to try to remove. It will certainly be useful to the family if she can help them see how they defeat their own ends with the authority figures they meet. This approach implies that the

[1] Waldron, F., "The Acceptance of Dependency in Social Casework", *Case Conference*, November, 1957.

worker has come to some understanding of her own authority and can appreciate the distinction, for example, between power and authority. Thus she may feel it appropriate to set some firm limits to some of the behaviour of problem families (to insist, for example, that the child goes to school regularly). Yet this insistence is not part of an exercise of general power over the family, and it is exercised in a spirit that makes it acceptable to the family. It is a product of the care the worker feels towards this family and an indication of her persisting concern that they continue as a family. The worker's attitude and the successful communication of her concern are the two essential elements in work with "problem families".

In this chapter a subject of wide dimensions and considerable social importance has been approached. Much of the problem has been only slightly indicated and much has been totally ignored. Only some very general principles or lines of approach have been suggested. These may assist the child care worker to establish meaningful contact with the family. A basic desire to be helpful is something, but it is insufficient if unaccompanied by the active demonstration that the casework actually brings some benefit. Once contact has been established on this basis the worker has to listen if she wishes to discover what the family needs.

> "In essence, it is the child himself and his family who tell the worker what kind of help is needed at any point in the child's development from pre-school age to adolescence."[1]

[1] Schwartz, A. C., "Some Developments in Family Casework on behalf of Children", *Social Casework*, Vol. XL, No. 8, October, 1959.

CHAPTER 8

THE CHILD CARE OFFICER

IT is a constant tendency of social work writing to set extremely high objectives for social work. This in turn affects workers in the field who may become depressed when they attempt to measure their own work by such a yardstick or who may dismiss critical consideration of their work as unnecessary and fruitless. It has been one of the major arguments of this book that casework should not be separated from the function of the agency offering social service. The argument of this final chapter is that objectives in casework must be seen in terms of the strains and stresses imposed on the caseworker by the job itself. In other words, we should begin to look at social work *as* work.[1]

No study so far published has been concerned with the Child Care Officer. It is the aim of this chapter to give some attention to the manifold responsibilities involved in the work of the child care officer, and to discuss some of the difficulties entailed in carrying them out. The discussion, in the absence of extensive practical research, is inevitably impressionistic, but it is concerned both to demonstrate likely areas for research in the future and also to call attention to some of the working problems of child care work.

(i) The Complex Roles of the Child Care Officer

We have already seen that the concept of "role" has an important part to play in the accurate and helpful description of human behaviour. It is also a notion that can usefully be applied in the attempt to describe social work. We can fruitfully ask what is the role of the social worker in the Child Care Service, for example.

---

[1] A beginning has been made in American writing in examining some of the stresses involved in practising social work. See Babcock, C. G., "The Social Worker in a World of Stress", *Social Service Review*, March, 1951; Babcock, C. G., "Social Work as Work", *Social Casework*, December, 1953; Feldman, Y., Spotnitz, H., and Nagelberg, L., "One Aspect of Casework Training through Supervision", *Social Casework*, April, 1953. The last contains a good discussion of the emotional impact of social work on the social worker.

By this term we refer to the behaviour that is expected of someone in the position of child care officer, to the feelings and attitudes that should be displayed and to the rewards that can legitimately be taken. These expectations are those of the child care officer herself and of those with whom she has contact in the course of her work. Such an approach is of particular relevance in the case of the child care officer because of the number and range of different kinds of people with whom she has contact simply because she is a child care officer. She works in the courts, presenting school reports in some areas, acting as the representative of the local authority, obtaining reports where juveniles are charged jointly with adults, etc. She collaborates with colleagues in residential work, with other local authority departments and with elected members. Her work is inspected by Home Office Inspectors and she has contact, spasmodic and sustained, with all kinds of statutory and voluntary social services. The most important aspects of her work involve her in relationships with natural and foster parents, with children and with residential staff.

In this situation the child care officer may easily feel she is pulled in many different directions and in fact may easily hold conflicting expectations of herself. Her role in any given relationship may be vague, or the expectations held may be unrealistic. The difficulties of enacting a role in which expectations may be fanciful, ambiguous or conflicting have been discussed recently by sociologists who have pointed out two separate kinds of difficulty.[1] The person faced with this situation may behave with too much caution, with uncertainty or ineffectively; and she may feel anxious and in conflict while she attempts to enact the role. In other words, the analysis of the child care officer's work in terms of the roles she has to play is not an academic exercise, but may well lead to an increased understanding of the strains and stresses of her job.

We ask, then, what expectations does the child care officer hold of herself and what do others expect of her? This sounds reasonably simple, but it is only as one tries to use the idea of expectation that its different meanings become clear. Expectation can refer to a person's view of the action he or another ought to perform in any particular role or it can refer to the kind of personal qualities they

[1] See *e.g.*, Sarbin, T. R., "Role Theory" in *Handbook of Social Psychology*, Vol. I, ed. Lindzey, G., Addison-Wesley, 1954, p. 227. Bernard, J., *Social Problems at Midcentury*, 1957.

should show. These two uses both concern expectation in the normative sense. Expectation can also be used to speak of what a person
thinks the role-taker (himself or another) will in fact do or what he
wishes he would do. In this chapter reference is made to expectation only in the normative sense, but future research should pay
attention to the two other strands of meaning, which have important
implications for the study of social work.

The first task in an analysis of expectation is to clarify what in
fact these expectations are. There are several sources for normative
expectations, the official regulations, writings on child care, the
policy of individual departments, the views of the professional
association and so on. In this chapter it will be possible to refer
only to three such sources, the official and "unofficial" literature
and the views of child care officers, foster parents and residential
staff as illustrated in a recent pilot study.[1]

The literature is not in itself extensive, but even a preliminary
review shows a list of specifications for the child care officer that
seems limitless and daunting. If we take the single task of selecting
foster homes as an example, we find the child care officer should:

find normal people[2]
discover the conscious and unconscious reasons for the application[3]
discover if the applicants are neurotic and reject if they are[4]
give foster parents insight into their application[5]
discover the foster parents' own needs and how they will try to satisfy
them[6]
assess the character of the foster parents and so on.[7]

This brief, arbitrary selection of role prescriptions should not, of
course, be seen as a cumulative list of expectations—no one person
expects a child care officer to do all these things. Yet some of the
expectations set goals which demand rare skills; the diagnosis, for
example, of the "neurotic" applicant. The list indicates that child
care officers are expected to perform difficult and differing tasks
which may demand different and possibly conflicting attitudes. In
brief, expectations as seen in the literature seem to be unrealistic
and sometimes unhelpful.

[1] Timms, N., and Itzin, F., "The Role of the Child Care Officer", *British Journal of Psychiatric Social Work*, Vol. VI, No. 2, 1961.
[2] Britton, C., *op. cit.*
[3] Balls, J., *op. cit.*, p. 143.
[4] Trasler, G., *op. cit.*, pp. 146, 148.
[5] *Ibid.*, p. 140.
[6] *Ibid.*, p. 238.
[7] Memorandum on the Boarding-out of Children Regulations, 1955, para. 35.

What are the other problems that might arise from the fact that the child care officer has to enact a number of roles? People may differ about the definition of a role and when two differing interpretations are offered there is the possibility of role conflict. Another kind of conflict may arise when the duties inherent in a role are clearly but insufficiently defined, or the possibilitity exists for different interpretations of the duties. Finally, there is the possibility of vagueness in role prescriptions. Examples of these three kinds of difficulty can be found in the literature.

In Chapter 6 the role of the child care officer in the supervision of foster homes was considered. It is difficult to give a precise definition of the behaviour and attitude expected of the worker in this situation, but it is possible to discover in the recent literature two completely different accounts. One writer, a child care officer, states

> "If potential foster-parents appear happy people, fond of each other and of their families, and if they show tolerance towards the type of child likely to be handed over to their care, they can probably be relied upon to make a success of the job with the minimum of interference from the visitor concerned."[1]

Here the child care officer is encouraged to leave the foster parents alone and to see her intervention in the situation as "interference". A sharply contrasting definition of the child care officer's role is given in another publication,

> "A child care officer who tries to withdraw from the foster home situation, under the impression that she is in some way spoiling the relationship between the foster parents and the child, is making a grave mistake. Unlike an ordinary family, which consists simply of parents and children, a foster family may be said to consist of foster parents, the child, his own parents, and the caseworker. The most successful placements which we studied were those in which both the foster parents and the caseworker recognized and understood this essential difference."[2]

This is a clear illustration of conflicting views about one of the worker's most important roles. Less clear, but equally important are the difficulties, often implicit, in regard to the child care officer's role in ensuring that foster children have a religious upbringing. The statutory regulation is definite on the point of religion and foster parents sign an undertaking that the child will be brought up in his own religion. Beyond this, however, there seems to be no indication of the worker's role in ensuring that this is done or in

---

[1] Balls, J., *op. cit.*, p. 144.   [2] Trasler, G., *op. cit.*, p. 235.

helping foster parents to carry out their obligations. It is, moreover, possible to interpret the idea of a religious upbringing in many different ways. Can one, for example, be said to bring up a child in his religious faith if one simply ensures that he attends his place of worship? This issue of religious upbringing will be considered more fully below, but it is raised here as an example of one of the child care officer's roles which is confused and ambiguous in spite of clear minimal statutory requirement.

Another role which sometimes produces difficulties when it is enacted is that contained in the duty imposed by s. 54 (3) of the Children Act, 1948, on local authorities "from time to time to cause children in voluntary homes in their area to be visited in the interests of the wellbeing of the children". Section 54 in general is concerned with the inspection of voluntary homes (by inspectors appointed by the Secretary of State), and in subsection (3) any person authorized to visit "in the interests of the well-being of the children" is given a right of entry. These two facts, and the feeling of the voluntary societies that their position in the field of child care is threatened by statutory "incursion", may often produce an unjustified aura of inspection around the visit of the individual child care officer in connection with a particular child. This confusion about role must often hinder effective communication.

There are, of course, other roles that are given by statute and regulation, but not very closely defined. For example, the Children Act of 1958 goes some way towards clarifying the role of the child care officer in regard to private foster homes. This is now defined as that of inspector and advice-giver (section 1), but it is doubtful how far the second role will evoke response in the private foster parent or enthusiasm in the child care worker.

Finally, some roles are not clearly defined by the regulations and are open to several differing interpretations. Perhaps the most striking example of this can be seen in rehabilitative work with the natural parents of children in care. Thus, the Seventh Report of the Children's Department of the Home Office states that:

> "it is recognised that committal to care . . . should be resorted to only where the influence of a skilled social worker could not reasonably be expected to effect the needed improvement, whether in the relationship of the parents with each other, in their care for the child, or in the child's behaviour."[1]

[1] Page 2.

Yet a judgment about what might reasonably be expected can be made only on the basis of attempts to do various things with and for the family. However valid and laudable the general objectives may be they certainly tend to confuse the role definition of the child care officer. With which families, and to what extent does she try to reach these objectives? To what extent is she expected to take on the family-centred role of the problem family worker, or the role of the marital counsellor, or that of the child guidance clinic worker? Does she perhaps take on all three roles and, in this case, are they compatible with each other and with her other work as a child care officer? The lack of clarity and the possibility of uncertainty and confusion are obvious.

This is a picture of the kinds of role problem that child care officers appear to face if we look at their work through existing literature and regulation. It is, of course, possible that such problems exist only in these sources and are not encountered in day-to-day work. What are the views of child care officers and of those with whom they establish working relationships?

There is little evidence on which to base an answer to this question, but a beginning has been made in a pilot investigation, which the author conducted with the collaboration of Professor Itzin of the School of Social Work, Iowa. In this study a small number of child care officers, foster mothers and residential staff was interviewed in an attempt to discover their expectation of the child care officer. The results showed that child care officers did not agree amongst themselves on some of the basic aspects of their role and that those with whom they worked had expectations of them which did not coincide with their views. Thus, in regard to work with children residential staff seemed to expect the child care officer to establish a direct relationship of trust with the child so that, if boarding-out broke down, the child would have someone to rely on. Child care officers, on the other hand, saw their work with children as minimal except in crises in the foster home, when they would discipline the child.

The full results of the study have been published elsewhere, but the general findings indicate that many of the problems of child care work stem from two important features of the child care officer's role. In the first place, she has to arrange for the care of children away from their parents. In other words, she is placed by the facts of her work in the role of successful competitor with natural parents. This is a situation that must cause varying degrees of emotional discomfort and make it difficult for the worker to form relationships with natural parents or with their children. To develop a personal relationship with children would make it seem that the child care officer had "taken" the children for herself. Consequently, the child must be given a new (foster) family as soon as possible and the child care officer must avoid as far as possible a relationship with him. Secondly, in a situation in which residential staff and foster parents can legitimately model their behaviour and attitudes on a parental model, the child care officer has no natural role to adopt.

The study also cast some light on the problem of the child care officer's role in the religious upbringing of the foster child. The general features of this problem have already been briefly outlined, but more attention can now be given to them. What is the role of the child care officer in securing that a foster child receives appropriate religious upbringing? The regulations are explicit on this point. The Boarding-Out Regulations, 1955, instruct the child care officer to obtain information on the religious persuasion of prospective foster parents and

> "where possible . . . (to board a child) with foster parents who either are of the same religious persuasion as the child or give an undertaking that he will be brought up in that religious persuasion" (reg. 19).

Yet once a child is boarded-out there seems to be no stipulation as to what the child care officer should do in regard to such upbringing; periodical reviews of boarded-out children are concerned only with "welfare, conduct, health and progress" (reg. 22). The absence of specific directions in regard to the boarded-out child is in marked contrast to the instructions in regard to the conduct of Children's Homes. A Memorandum by the Home Office on Children's Homes (1951) states that

> "A child who has to grow up away from his own parents needs even more than any other the comfort and help of a religious faith . . . A religious upbringing must be founded on the example of the people with whom a child lives; if they are sincere in their convictions, even though of a different denomination, the teaching and guidance that he receives will have added significance . . . The housemother should be ready to discuss with any child religious or other questions which he may raise, and where desirable to arrange for him to talk with a

minister of religion or other adviser of his own persuasion with whom
it is hoped she will maintain friendly contact" (paras. 15, 16).

There is, thus, an interesting lack of symmetry between what is
required of workers in residential and in field positions on this topic
of religion.

This lack of symmetry is due partly to the complexity of the
problems that arise once it is agreed that the child care officer has
some responsibility to ensure that a child in a foster home is receiving
an appropriate religious upbringing. Is such responsibility based on
the rights of parents, on the special religious needs of the deprived
child, or on the general assumption that all children ought to receive
a religious upbringing or on some combination of one or more of
these assumptions? The general physical and moral well-being of
children has been accepted as an aim of the Education Service, but
once an attempt is made to translate this into specific acts and
obligations considerable difficulties are encountered. What is the
position in the practice of child care?

Again, there is hardly any evidence based on observed fact, but
the results of the pilot study already mentioned are certainly
suggestive. The three groups interviewed, foster parents, residential
staff and child care officers were presented with the following
situation:

> "A nine-year-old boy is fostered with parents of a different religion
> to his own. They attend their place of worship irregularly. The boy
> begins to stay away from his church and the minister informs the
> child care officer."

Respondents were asked what the child care officer should find out
about this situation and what action she should take. The foster
mothers were clear and uniform in thinking that the child should
attend church and that the child care officer should encourage the
foster parents to set an example. One foster mother added that the
child care officer never enquired about the foster child's religious
practice and that it would do no harm for her to do so. Responses
from the child care officers covered a considerable range from denial
that a problem existed, through believing that the solution rested in
the boy's own decision or that the minister should handle the situation, to holding a frank discussion with the foster parents.

These results cannot be generalized, but they indicate the possibility of a wide range of practice. The problem requires both

theoretical analysis and further empirical investigation. At the moment it is covered by the decent obscurity of silence, but the ultimate issues are whether the rights of parents and children are sufficiently protected by the vague stress on the religious upbringing of the foster child and whether such an upbringing should be made a reality?

These, then, are some of the problems facing the child care officer in terms of role conflict and role uncertainty. Other problems stem from staff relationships within the service and to the emotional stresses of the work.

(ii) Staff Relationships

The Child Care Service was established in 1948 to deal with urgent problems revealed after a period (the 1920's and 30's) of fairly general stagnation in respect of residential care and of several branches of casework. It is a service established in the setting of local authority, subject to the regulations and customs of that world. This in itself often presents a newcomer to the service with some problems of adjustment. The Service was, moreover, seen in its early days, and in varying degrees today, as a threat to well-established interests in such Departments as those of Education and Health. The child care officer has to learn how to co-operate with workers in all Departments in a way that faces the power politics of local government. It is all too easy for diplomacy to give way to indignation.

There are, of course, strains within Departments. These can be seen in terms of differences in role definition. For example, does the Children's Officer see himself purely as an administrator, or also as a casework supervisor? If he values administrative performance (partly because it can be clearly seen, partly because of the desire for a reputation for efficiency) does he encourage his field staff to divorce casework completely from administrative procedures, to the ultimate cost of both? Strain is implicit, too, in the structure of the service from the point of view of personnel. The service is staffed by people with many different kinds of training, or no training at all, for the job they are doing. In the field, staff may be untrained, may have had a professional child care training or may simply hold a social science diploma, which should in many respects be considered no training at all. Only 25% of child care officers hold a professional social work qualification, and only 9% of residential staff employed by local authorities have been trained on house parents courses. In some voluntary societies, however, the proportion is very much higher.[1] There is, moreover, a high turnover of staff in local authorities and this, combined with the fact that many young and inexperienced social science students can easily obtain posts in Children's Departments, must increase the burdens on staff members who stay longer.

Perhaps the most difficult of the problems facing child care officers within their departments is their relationship to staff working in residential settings. Again, this can be seen in terms of role; what are the respective roles of field and residential staff?

At the beginning of the service considerable emphasis was, as we have seen, given to boarding-out. This had personal repercussions since residential staff felt excluded from any participation in decisions about which child was to be boarded-out, especially if they had become attached to the individual child in question. This difficulty can still arise and may sometimes complicate the child's problem.

> Geraldine (13), for example, was placed after a foster home breakdown in a voluntary children's home. She was referred to a psychiatrist because of the behaviour that had precipitated the foster home breakdown, and he advised that she be placed in a school for maladjusted children. In the meantime the child care worker was urging Geraldine to continue visits to the foster home. When Geraldine was taken to see a school for maladjusted children she remarked that the matron of the Children's Home could not see why she had to be moved and had told her she was going to see "a daft school".

In this particular case a young worker had sensed the criticism of the voluntary home staff, and had managed most of the arrangements by letter. Personal contact with the staff, though difficult, might have shown them that they were not regarded as a "dumping-ground" for foster home failures, and might have gained some active co-operation from them, so that Geraldine would not have been confused about the sort of school she was being sent to. It would also have stopped Geraldine attempting to play off worker against residential staff.

In general, however, it seems that considerable effort is now made

---

[1] For an account, somewhat anecdotal, of developments in training residential staff in the National Children's Homes, see Wilson, A., *Progress in Child Care*.

to bring together these two sides of the service. The Home Office, for example, now arranges joint refresher courses for field and residential staff. Child care officers are now more aware of the feelings of residential staff, of the necessity of consulting them at the planning stage, and of the value of their knowledge of the child. Residential workers perhaps feel less threatened by the fieldworker, and have less need to feel envious of the child care officer's car and less restricted working life.

Yet serious problems remain. In the social services as a whole the place of residential care has not been clearly defined. There is a fairly strongly held view that institutions as such are bad. Vaizey, for instance, states that everyone

> "longs for the day when the last children's home is burnt to the ground. But the same is not the case for the sick, the old, the mad or the criminal. These places are all fantastically more expensive than ordinary life and their results are harmful, socially and psychologically."[1]

In this climate of opinion, it is unlikely that institutions will attract staff of sufficient calibre or be encouraged to think out afresh their specialized contribution to social welfare. We have so far in this country given residential staff neither status nor knowledge to develop their specific tasks in specialized treatment centres. In the past they have often been seen as "holding" establishments whilst other staff, usually extra-mural, actually "treat", but the residential setting should provide more than a roof and food. The experience of living in a specially structured environment should become of itself a main therapy.

Residential staff in Children's Homes have to face not only the implications of these attitudes, but special difficulties in their work with other people's children. The more these can be appreciated by the child care officer, the more successful her co-operation with residential staff will be. They are, moreover, difficulties the officer has to face in her own work in the field. Part of the difficulty in the way of increased co-operation is to be found in the child care officer's own feelings that in boarding-out children from residential Homes she is once again breaking-up "a family" (that of child and residential staff).

In a residential setting workers are often brought into contact

---

[1] Vaizey, J., *Scenes from Institutional Life*, 1959, p. 107.

11*

with the parents of the children for whom they care, and exposed to the impact of these parents' feelings against those who actually have the day-by-day handling of their children. Thus they meet neglectful parents who are angrily critical of the physical care the child receives, parents who are unable to bear the apparent good behaviour of their children in the hands of other people. It is not always easy to see their anger and hostile behaviour as a mask for feelings of inadequacy and despair.

Residential workers in child care must sometimes feel that they are left with the children nobody else wants, those who cannot be boarded-out or who have failed in foster homes. Sometimes the value or lack of value placed by society on those with whom we habitually work rubs off onto us. Moreover, residential staff are increasingly called on to care for those who may be or actually are maladjusted. This tendency may increase under the new Mental Health Act. Section 9(3) of the Act states that nothing in any enactment shall prevent a local authority from receiving into care a child who is mentally disordered. Section 9(1) states that a children's authority may accommodate in their Homes or elsewhere any child who is not in care, but whose care or after-care is being undertaken by any local health authority under arrangements for persons who are or have been suffering from mental disorder.

This development raises in an important way the question of the role of the caseworker in her relationship with residential staff. If the staff are already called on to help with numbers of disturbed children, are there not ways in which they can be helped with the problems this entails by the fieldwork staff? In the pilot study already referred to fieldworkers and residential staff emphasized that they expected information from each other, but does this exhaust the possibilities? Some caseworkers who have been appointed to residential agencies have experienced the difficulties of proceeding beyond this point, but they have also shown how much help the fieldworker can give in the handling of children found difficult if she concentrates on trying to understand the specific problem that any particular child presents to the worker concerned.[1] Help based on this understanding is not offered from the standpoint of superiority,

[1] For some useful reflections on this theme see Irvine, E. E., "Two Approaches to Adjustment Problems among children in Institutions", *British Journal of Psychiatric Social Work*, November, 1951.

but from a difference in training and a vantage point different from that occupied by the residential worker.

(iii) Emotional Implications

In Chapter 7 we saw some of the distressing family situations with which the child care officer is concerned. These are families in which the parents are extremely needful, and the fear and anger and sadness they feel is easily conveyed to the social worker. The day-to-day problems and crises in these families may involve the worker in an intricate net of communications with other agencies, who will sometimes project onto her some of their resentment against these families. The worker may meet very serious cases of marital difficulties, parent–child relationships and the pathology of individual members. She has to face them when she has responsibility (in a county) for a large area involving considerable travelling, and when the state of our knowledge about such families is practically non-existent. She has, however, some support from the notion that she is trying to keep a family intact, even though the progress of her work may be seen only over a time-span of years.

In other cases she is involved directly or indirectly in the break-up of a family, in the separation of child and parent. This situation involves her in a role relationship with the court, which demands evidence of a kind different from that on which she might make a casework judgment. It also involves her own deep feelings about taking children away from their parents. Child care has a long tradition of encouraging a rescue policy; children were living in physical, moral and social squalor, and it was the duty of the child care worker to remove the child and see that it was cared for in a clean, respectable, Christian environment. The emphasis on the squalor of the natural home was an expression of pity for children and of disgust at their parents, but today we have increasingly come to recognize that parents have feelings for their children even when they neglect them. This has presented child care workers with a new problem of guilt.

Undoubtedly we find difficulty in sharing the care of children with the natural parents and with colleagues in the residential setting or, for example, at the Child Guidance Clinic. This in turn creates problems for the child, but we often appear to deal with this sharing problem by blaming the parents or by treating them as children who have to be humoured if they create a nuisance but who are basically without rights in the situation. The sort of attitude this focus encourages can be seen in the following quotation from a Children's Department Report:

> "contact between parents and children who are boarded-out raises much more difficult problems, for most boarded-out children have been committed to the care of the local authority or are children in respect of whom parental rights have been assumed. This almost always means that the parents have proved themselves unfit to look after the children—in which case it is very unlikely that they would be acceptable as visitors in the foster home. In fact, in practically every such case it is necessary to keep the whereabouts of the children from the parents, and arrange such contacts as do take place in some 'neutral' place such as the department's office. A number of parents do regularly meet their children in this way and even take them out for half-day outings; and the *privilege* (my italics) has not been abused. On the other hand, there have been children, living in happy and respectable foster homes, who have come increasingly to dislike meeting parents who make no effort to keep themselves clean and wholesome, and have asked that all contact should cease. Where the children have obviously been old enough to make such a decision with a sense of responsibility, and where the parents have obviously made no effort to rehabilitate themselves, the committee have agreed to such requests."[1]

This extract is taken from a report published in 1953 and actual practice has probably changed. However, what is important for present purposes is the attitude displayed towards the parents. It is, of course, extremely difficult to work in a Children's Department without becoming child-centred. This is partly because the aim of the work is to help children and also because workers enter the service motivated to this end. Workers in other fields have shown how difficult it is to have continuous regard for the whole family when in fairly intense contact with one family member. Yet our increased understanding of the psychological importance of the family as a whole imposes the responsibility of correcting the bias of interest in favour of the single family member. To treat the parents of neglected children as completely incompetent, to blame them for their neglect is ultimately to render disservice to the children. For, however neglected, the children carry within themselves images and, as it were, parts of their parents and to blame the parents is to appear to blame the children. A beginning can be made in rectifying the balance if it is recognized that we tend to blame parents not necessarily because we are censorious

---

[1] The First Four Years (cited at p. 22, *ante*), p. 40.

people with small sympathies, but because we are anxious at separating children from their parents and deal with this anxiety by the attachment of blame to other people.

The child care worker must often have doubts about the effectiveness of her work. This is perhaps true for all social workers, but especially for the child care worker at the present time, when so much emphasis is placed on the crucial importance for later development of experiences in the early years of life. Work with any particular child often begins with considerable handicaps. We are in every case, after all, offering "a substitute". Bennett, for example, in a study of delinquent and neurotic children, draws attention to the treble handicap under which we work when normal home life has failed, and we attempt to find a substitute. She states that these foster homes, hostels, etc., offer a

> "socializing and corrective influence, even when most wisely and kindly administered, (which) comes *after* there has been a deeply inscarred original failure, often publicly recognized; that these 'secondary homes' to which the child is transplanted operate at least within a second-hand authority system which has weakened human attachments and diluted emotional meaning and is, therefore, a shallower soil for the child's roots than his 'own' home; and thirdly that very often this 'second chance' in social adaptation is offered *so many years too late*."[1]

This is a depressing statement that truly reflects aspects of the work of child care which must be faced. Yet it provides no licence for despair. We know from experience that many children can be helped to overcome the obstacles to happiness that undoubtedly exist, and that we can achieve limited but real success in helping parents and children to enjoy life and each other. A true grasp of the magnitude and multitude of the problems they face is an essential preliminary to real help. We know also that in many cases we may fail, but we could not know this beforehand in any particular case. Even when the chances of success of a modified kind seem remote all our skill must be used,

> "Not for the good that it will do
> But that nothing may be left undone
> On the margin of the impossible."[2]

[1] Bennett, J., *Delinquent and Neurotic Children*, 1960, p. 225.
[2] Eliot, T. S., *The Family Reunion*, 1939, p. 34.

ADDITIONAL READING

GENERAL:

Articles

Castle, M.—"Casework and Child Care", *Child Care*, Vol. VII, No. 3, July, 1953.

Freeman L.—"The Child and the Local Authority",*Child Care*,Vol. XIV, No. 4, October, 1960.

Jehu, D.—"Relationships in Child Care", *Child Care*, Vol. XIV, No. 3, July, 1960.

Kahn, A. J.—"Can the Effectiveness of Child Care be Determined?", *Child Welfare*, Vol. XXXIII, No. 2, February, 1954.

FOSTER CARE:

Books

Dyson, D. M.—*The Foster Home and the Boarded-Out Child*, Allen and Unwin, 1947.

Kaplan, L. K.—*Foster-Home Placement, in Psycho-Analysis and Social Work*, ed. M. Heiman, International University Press, 1953.

Mordy, I.—*The Child Wants a Home*, Harrap, 1956.

Theis, S. V. S.—*How Foster Children Turn Out*, State Charities Aid Association, New York, 1924.

Articles and Pamphlets

Aptekar, H.—"Three Aspects of the Role of the Worker in Homefinding", *Child Welfare*, Vol. XXIII, No. 1, January, 1944.

Charnley, J.—"Helping Foster-Parents to Achieve Satisfaction", Casework Papers, 1955, Family Service Association, America.

Cole, L. C.—"The Triangle in Child Placement", *Social Service Review*, June, 1951.

Crystal, D.—"What Keeps us from Giving Children what they Need?", *Social Service Review*, Vol. XXVII, No. 2, June, 1953.

Kline, D.—"Understanding and Evaluating a Foster Family's Capacity to Meet the Needs of an Individual Child",*Social Service Review*,Vol. XXXIV, No. 2, June, 1960.

Kline, D., and Littner, N.—*Casework with Foster Parents*, Child Welfare League of America, 1956.

Littner, N.—"The Child's Need to Repeat His Past, Some Implications for Placement", *Social Service Review*, June, 1960.

Meier, E. G.—"The Needs of Adolescents in Foster Care", *Child Welfare*, Vol. XXXVII, No. 3, April, 1958.

Naughton, F.—"Foster-Home Placement as an Adjunct to Residential Treatment", *Social Casework*, Vol. XXXVIII, No. 6, June, 1957.

Silberpfennig, J., and Thornton, E.—"Preparation of Children for Placement", *The Family*, Vol. XXIII, No. 4, June, 1942.

Weisenbarger, R.—"Direct Casework with the Child in Foster-Home Placement", *Child Welfare (U.S.A.)*, Vol. XXX, No. 4, April, 1951.

Williams, J. M.—"Children who break down in Foster-Homes", *Journal of Child Psychology and Psychiatry*, June, 1961.

Wires, E.—"Long-time Care in a Public Child-Placing Agency", *Social Casework*, Vol. XXXII, No. 5, May, 1951.

Wires, E.—"Some Factors in the Worker Foster-Parent Relationship", *Child Welfare*, Vol. XXXIII, No. 8, October, 1954.

Wolins, M.—"Workers' Decisions in Foster Home Finding", *Child Welfare*, Vol. XXXVIII, No. 9, November, 1959.

CHILDREN AND ADOLESCENTS:

Articles

Beck, B.—"The Adolescent's Challenge to Casework", *Social Work (U.S.A.)*, April, 1958.

Baugham, W. R.—"Casework with Children Committed against their Will", *Child Welfare*, Vol. XXIV, No. 10, December, 1945.

Hirsohn, S.—"The Role of the Male Caseworker with the Adolescent Boy", *Social Casework*, Vol. XXXI, No. 1, January, 1950.

Josselyn, I.—"Psychological Problems of the Adolescent", *Social Casework*, Vol. XXXII, Nos. 5 and 6, May and June 1951.

Matthews, J.—"Casework Treatment of Two Motherless Adolescent Girls", *Social Casework*, Vol. XXXV, No. 8, October, 1954.

Ross, H.—"The Caseworker and the Adolescent", *The Family*, November, 1941.

Welsch, E. E.—"Sustaining the Child in his Impaired Home", *Child Welfare*, Vol. XXXII, No. 7, July, 1953.

FAMILIES:

Articles and Pamphlets

Beck, B. M.—"Protective Casework Revitalized", *Child Welfare*, Vol. XXXIV, Nos. 9 and 10, November and December, 1955.

Behrens, M. L. and Ackerman.—"The Home Visit as an Aid in Family Diagnosis and Therapy", *Social Casework*, Vol. XXXVII, No. 1, January, 1956.

Carlebach, J.—"Parents of Children in Care", *Child Care*, Vol. XIV, No. 3, July, 1960.

Glickman, E.—"Treatment of the Child and his Family after Placement", *Social Service Review*, Vol. XXVIII, No. 3, September, 1954.

Hill, R.—"Social Stresses on the Family", *Social Casework*, Vol. XXXIX, Nos. 2 and 3, February-March, 1958.

Irvine, E. E.—"Some Notes on Problem Families and Immaturity", *Case Conference*, March, 1960.

Kline, D.—"Service to Parents of Placed Children, Some Changing Problems and Goals", *Social Service Review*, Vol. XXXIV, No. 2, June, 1960.

Laufer, M. L.—"Casework with Parents: Our Obligation to their Adolescents in Placement", *Child Welfare*, Vol. XXXII, No. 9, November, 1953.

Overton, A., and Tinker, K.—*Casework Notebook*, St. Paul, Minnesota.

Rall, R. E.—"The Casework Process in Work with the Child and the Family in the Child's Own Home", *Social Service Review*, Vol. XXVIII, No. 3, September, 1954.

Roach, J. L.—"Helping Families who Don't Want Help", *Public Welfare*, Vol. XVII, No. 2, April, 1959.

THE CHILD CARE OFFICER:

Littner, L.—*The Strains and Stresses on the Child Welfare Worker*, Child Welfare League of America, 1957.

INDEX

A

ADEQUACY
  foster parents, 102
    illustration, 102
  problems, 118
ADMISSION TO CARE, 21 *et seq.*
  application for, 22–23. *And see*
    APPLICATION
  work of child care officer, 22
ADOLESCENTS
  anxieties, 69
  casework with, 59 *et seq.*
  development, 61
  families, importance, 68–71
  helping, 59 *et seq.*
  illustrations, 63, 70, 72, 73, 74, 76
  independence, desire for, 69, 70
           fear of, 70
  knowledge of, 59
  parents and, conflict, 62
          relationship, 60
  phases, 61
  problems, 60
      behaviour, 73
      conscience, 62, 71–74
      identity, 61–62, 74–75
      money, 70
      opportunities, 77
      standards, 72
      taking help, 76
  removal from families, 70–71
  variety among, 60
  worker, dependence on, 76
      relationship with, 70
AFTER-CARE SUPERVISION, 70
AGENCY FUNCTION, 127, 145
  co-operation, 140, 141
      illustration, 141
  explanation to client, 25
  financial, 142–143
  problem families, 135
AINSWORTH, M., 85
ALBEMARLE REPORT, 77
ALMONERS
  original objectives, 4
AMBIVALENCE, 15, 130
ANXIETY
  work with adolescents, in, 78
APPELL, G., 85

APPLICATION
  admission to care for—
    appraisal, 23–24
    identification of problem, 29
    illustrations, 24–25, 27, 31
    questions, 27
APPRAISAL
  casework in, 7 *et seq.*
APPROVED SCHOOL MAN-
  AGERS, 70
ASHDOWN, M., 9
AUBRY, J., 85

B

BABCOCK, C. G., 145
BALLS, J., 147, 148
BAXTER, A., 86
BEHAVIOUR
  as expression of anxiety, 76
BEHAVIOUR STANDARDS
  outline by worker, 73
BENNETT, J., 159
BERNARD, J., 146
BERNSTEIN, A., 20
BIBLIOGRAPHY, 161
BIRCHALL, J. D., 81
BIRMINGHAM
  Children's Department Report, 22,
    80, 88, 126–127, 158
BOARDING-OUT, 57, 79 *et seq.*
  effect on adolescents, 69
  Regulations, 1955...84, 94, 107, 151
          Memorandum, 68,
             107, 147

  And see FOSTER CARE
BOSANQUET, HELEN, 3, 10, 12, 22
BOWEN, ELIZABETH, 48
BOWLBY, J., 23, 45, 84, 85, 87
BREAK UP
  family. *See* PREVENTION
BRITTON, CLARE, 9, 36, 68, 75, 92,
    109, 147

BROUGH, R., 79
BURLINGHAM, D., 85
BURT, C., 14

C

CARE
  admission to, 21
  committal to, by courts, 33 *et seq.*
CARPENTER, Mary, 38, 39
CASEWORK
  adolescents with, 59 *et seq.*
  children, with, 38 *et seq.*, 58
    criticisms, 40
    illustrations, 41
    uses, 41
  definitions, 2
  description, 3
  history, 3 *et seq.*
  relation to statutory obligations, 5
  "scientific" laws, 11
CASEWORKER. *See* WORKER
CHALMERS, 7
CHARITY ORGANIZATION
  SOCIETY, 4, 6, 7, 10, 11, 14, 18,
  95, 143
  Annual Report, 1915–16...2
             1933–34...39
  Occasional Papers, 1918...1
CHILDCARE,
  policy changes, 104
CHILD CARE OFFICER. *See*
  WORKER
CHILD CARE SERVICE
  history, 153
CHILD GUIDANCE, 30
CHILDREN
  admission to care, 21 *et seq.*
  casework with—
    early, 39
    illustrations, 41, 51–56
    play activity, 49
    purpose, 49–50
  caseworker, relationship with, 47
  committed to care, 21, 126
  development, 42 *et seq.*
  early years, importance, 159
  identity, establishment of, 45
  parents, relationship with, 46–48
        returning to, 131–134
  received into care, 21
  understanding of, 43 *et seq.*
  worth, establishment of, 45
CHILDREN ACT, 1948...21, 22, 33,
  54, 79, 81, 126, 129, 132, 149
CHILDREN ACT, 1958...149

CHILDREN AND YOUNG PER-
  SONS (AMENDMENT) ACT,
  1952...70
CHILDREN'S DEPARTMENT
  admission to care by, 21 *et seq.*
  family care provided by, 23
  function, explanation of, 32
  relevance of casework to, 2
  Seventh Report, 80
CHILDREN'S HOME, 36
  staff. *See* RESIDENTIAL STAFF
CLIENT
  caseworker and, relationship, 17
  psychiatric social worker and, re-
    lationship, 18 *et seq.*
COLE, L. C., 109
COLEMAN, R. W. 40
COMMITTAL
  care, to, by courts, 33 *et seq.*
COMMUNICATION
  casework with children, in, 48–49
  difficulties, 10, 76
  worker and prospective foster parents,
    99
CONSCIENCE
  problems of, adolescents', 71–74
CONTINUITY
  Children's Department as providing,
    75
CONTROL
  adolescents, of, 76
  foster parents, problems of, 104–106
CO-OPERATION, 140
COSENS, M., 9, 39
COURT
  committal to care by, 21, 33 *et seq.*
  order, 124
  worker's role, 157
CURTIS COMMITTEE
  Report, 82, 92

D

DAVISON, E., 2
DENNIS, N., 13
DEPENDENCE, 76
  financial, 142–143
DEPRIVATION
  effects of, 73, 75
  maternal, 23, 84
DEVELOPMENT
  stages of, 48, 84
DIAGNOSIS
  casework in, 7 *et seq.*, 84

DONNISON, D. V., 140
DORAN, M., 82

E

EASTON, R., 134, 142
EDUCATION SERVICE, 152, 153
ELIOT, T. S., 159
ELKAN, I., 125–126
EMOTIONAL PROBLEMS
  worker, of, 157–159
ENVIRONMENT
  problem families, 136
ERIKSON, E. H., 48
EXPECTATION
  definition, 146

F

FAMILIES
  adolescents—
    effect of absence on, 69
    importance to, 68
    removal from, 70–71
  as a whole, 139
  break-up. *See* PREVENTION
  early casework with, 39
  members of, work with, 32
  responsibility of, 30
  separation from, 23
  work with, 54, 124 *et seq.*
  See also PROBLEM FAMILIES
FATHERS
  neglected in social work, 13, 140
FELDMAN, Y., 145
FINANCE
  assistance with, 142–143
  Children's Department regulations,
    142
  contributions, 126
    collection, 127
    illustration, 128
  problems—
    help with, 142
    problem families, 136
FISHER, D. W., 89*n.*
"FIT"
  role and personality, 139–140
FIT PERSON ORDER, 80*n.*
FOSTER CARE
  breakdown, 115
  child, specific, discussion with pro-
    spective parents, 95
  Children's Departments, pressure on,
    80, 95

FOSTER CARE—*continued*
  economic advantages, 80
  policy, changes, 81
  religion, 148–149
  social history of child, 91
  worker's role—
    complexity, 81
    inspectoral, 81–82
  And see SHORT-STAY FOSTERING
FOSTER CHILD
  parents and, relationship, 101, 108
    natural, contact with, 104
  placement, illustration, 91
  worker and, relationship, 101
FOSTER HOME
  breakdown, 108
  selection, worker's tasks, 147
  shortage, 95
  supervision—
    by worker, literature, 148
    illustration, 115 *et seq.*
FOSTER MOTHER
  response to visitor, 110
  And see FOSTER PARENTS
FOSTER PARENTS, 36, 53, 55–56,
  79 *et seq.*
  age, 87
  application—
    anxieties, 96
    consideration, 88
    criminal record, 95
    first interview, 98
    flexibility, 90
    future stresses, 91
    illustrations, 96, 98
    indirect request for help, 109
    motive, 89, 90
    "neurotic", 89
    rejection, 100
    response to worker, 92, 93
    state of family, 92
    understanding of, 93
    worker, relationship with, 93
      skill, 93 *et seq.*
      statutory duty, 94
  casework principles, 115
  child and, relationship, 101, 108
  choice of, 82, 83 *et seq.*, 86, 88
  expectations, 87
  financial benefits, 89
  knowledge of, limited, 87
  natural parents and, 103
  negative feelings, 115
  neighbours, 102
  problems, 83, 101 *et seq.*
    adequacy, 102, 118
    control, 104–106
    emotional significance, 111

FOSTER PARENTS—*continued*
  problems—*continued*
    help with, 106
    hostility, 113
    illustrations, 104, 105, 110, 119
      et seq.
    natural parents, 118
    preparation for, 105–106
    rivalry, 103
    sharing, 104
    worker's attitude, 106
  rejection, 83
  religion, 151
  routine visiting, 115
  worker and, relationship, 83, 101,
      107, 109, 111
    illustrations, 111–114, 119 *et seq.*
  worker, image of, 108
      communication with, 99
FRAIBURG, S., 38
FREUD, A., 20, 47, 85, 131
"FRIENDLY VISITOR", 17, 18

G

GARDNER, G. E., 86
GLASGOW
  boarding-out rate, 79
GLICKMAN, E., 83, 109
GOLDBERG, E. M., 71
GOLDFARB, W., 23, 85
GOLDING, L., 43
GORDON, H., 50, 95
GRAHAM, J. A. D., 6
GRAY, P. G., 80, 87
GURSLLIN, O., 13

H

HEALTH SERVICE, 153
HERO-WORSHIP, 76
HEYWOOD, J. S., 40, 79
HILL, OCTAVIA, 1, 14, 19
HISTORY, SOCIAL. *See* SOCIAL
  HISTORY
HITCHMAN, J., 43
HOLLINGSHEAD, A. B., 13
HOLMAN, J., 10
HOME OFFICE
  Children's Department, 6th Report,
      34
      7th Report,
      149

HOME OFFICE—*continued*
  Memorandum on Children's Homes,
      1957...151
  refresher courses, 155
HOWRER, M., 87
HUMAN RELATIONS
  seminars, 128
  skill in, 16
HUNT, R. G., 13
HUTCHINSON, D., 83

I

IDENTITY
  problems of, 74–75
ILLUSTRATIONS
  adequacy, foster parents, 102
  adolescent, 63, 70, 72–74, 76
  agency co-operation, 141
  application for admission to care,
      24–25, 27, 31
  casework with children, 41, 51–56
  children committed to care, 35
  foster child placement, 91
      home supervision, 115 *et seq.*
      parent and worker relation-
          ship, 111–114, 119 *et*
          seq.
          application, 96, 98
          problems, 104, 105, 110,
          119 *et seq.*
  maladjusted child, 119 *et seq.*
  parent and child, keeping apart, 70
      inconsistency, 129
      recognition as, 125
      regaining care of child, 132, 133
  recreation of past, 44
  referral to another agency, 16
  residential staff problems, 154
IMMATURITY
  problem families, 137
INFANTS
  casework with, 50
INGLEBY REPORT, 142
INITIATIVE
  problems of, 75
INSPECTION
  statutory, 149
INSPECTORS, 146
INSTITUTIONS
  adverse views, 155
  relationships with staff, 57
INTROJECTION, 46
INVESTIGATION, 84
  casework in, 7 *et seq.*
  foster parents, suitability, 94

INVESTIGATION—*continued*
method of, 10
preliminary to relief, 1, 7
treatment and, 8
IRVINE, E. E., 137, 156
ISAACS, S., 87
ITZIN, F., 147, 150

J

JEALOUSY
foster parents, 103
JEWISH BOARD OF GUARDIANS,
7
JOSSALYN, L., 59, 90
JUNG, 14, 15

K

KELLY, E. L., 89*n*.
KERR, M., 13
KLEIN, M., 46
KRIS, E., 40

L

LAURENCE, K. L., 8
LENNARD, H., 20
LEWIS, H., 23, 85
LLOYD, K., 47
LOCAL AUTHORITY
duty in fostering, 81
LOCAL GOVERNMENT BOARD
Report, 1891/2...101
1892/3...81
LOCH, C. S., 4, 11, 12
LOGAN, R. F., 71
LONDON GOVERNMENT BOARD
Report, 1891/2...82, 101

M

MALADJUSTED CHILDREN, 156
illustration, 119 *et seq.*
school, 122–123
MARRIAGE
problems, effect on children, 131
MENTAL HEALTH ACT, 1959...156
MENTAL HYGIENE MOVEMENT,
39
MILNES, N., 2
MOTHER
"rejecting," 131

MOTIVES
effect on actions, 90
foster parents, 89, 90
MUNDELLA COMMITTEE
Poor Law Schools, 82
Report, 89
MYERS, E., 17

N

NAGELBERG, L., 145
NATIONAL ASSISTANCE BOARD,
128
NEWELL, H. W., 131
NORMALITY, 113–114

O

OEDIPUS COMPLEX, 47
definition, 15
OMNIPOTENCE, 26*n*.

P

PACIFIST SERVICE UNIT, 142
PARENTS
adolescents and, conflicts, 62
relationship, 60, 62
applicants for care, 26
children committed to care, of, 34, 35
deprived of child, guilt, 125
disturbed personalities, 129
inconsistency, illustration, 129
influence on children, 40
natural, children's attitude in foster
care, 86
part played by, 75
recognition as, 125
illustration, 125
regaining care of children, 131–134
child's behaviour, 133
decision, 132
illustrations, 132, 133
worker's attitude, 133
relationship with children, 46–48
retaining care of children, 134
separated from child—
concept of worker, 127
contact, 126
financial contributions, 126
illustration, 70
keeping apart, 128, 130
needs, 127
worker as competitor, 151
attitude, 157–158
PARR, E. A., 80, 87

PAST
   recreation of, 44, 45, 86
PIGOU, A. C., 18
PLAY ACTIVITY, 49
POOR LAW AUTHORITIES, 4
   Mundella Committee, 82
PREVENTION
   definitions, 134
   specialist workers, 135
PROBATION, 139
PROBLEM FAMILIES, 141
   economics, 136
   environment, 136
   help, offers, 142
   immaturity, 137
   literature, 135
   relationships, 137
      authority, 143
      children, 142
      outside groups, 138
      worker, 138
   social position, 138
   worker's attitude, 144
PROJECTION, 46, 71
PROFESSION
   qualifications, 154
PROFESSIONAL BEHAVIOUR, 9,
   112
PROVIDENT DISPENSARIES, 4
PROVINCE, S., 40
PSYCHIATRY. See SOCIAL WORKER,
   psychiatric
PSYCHO-ANALYSIS
   adolescents, treatment of, 69
   concepts, value of, 15, 16
   early casework in, 14
   history of casework in, 12
PSYCHOLOGY
   casework interpretation in, 11
   early casework in, 14
   influence of, 8
   understanding of individual in, 12

R

RAPOPORT, R., 139
RECEPTION
   children in care, of, 34
RECREATION
   past, of, 44, 45, 86
REDLICH, M. D., 13
REHABILITATION, 131–134, 149
REJECTION, 100, 131

RELIGION, 107
   basis of responsibility, 152
   foster child, range of opinions, 152
      statutory provisions, 151
   parents, 94, 148–149
      worker's role, 151
RESIDENTIAL STAFF
   parents' feelings, 156
   problems, illustration, 154
   role, undefined, 155
   worker and, relationship, 150, 154,
      156
   co-operation, 155
RETICENCE
   lack of, 130
REYNOLDS, B., 82
RIVALRY
   foster parents, 103, 110
ROACH, J. L., 13
ROLE
   sociological concept, 13
ROSENBLUTH, D., 85
ROSOW, I., 139

S

SARBIN, T. R., 146
SCHOOL
   effect on child, 141
   staff, relationship with worker, 141
SCHWARTZ, A. C., 144
SELECT COMMITTEE ON ESTI-
   MATES
   Report, 80
SEPARATION
   effects of, 85
   parents from children, 124
   psychological problems, 85
SHARING
   foster care, in, 103, 104
   problem families, 137
SHORT-STAY FOSTERING, 80
SOCIAL AGENCY
   client's understanding of, 6
   function, 4
   referral to another, 16
      illustration, 16 et seq.
   use of casework in, 4 et seq.
SOCIAL CLASS
   studies, 13
SOCIAL HISTORY
   child in care, of, 34
      of, relating to needs, 36
   early, later value of, 9

SOCIAL HISTORY—*continued*
foster child, placement, in, 91
process of obtaining, 9
use of, 44, 87, 125
SOCIAL INSTITUTIONS
problem families, 138
SOCIAL WORK
criticism of, 10
SOCIAL WORKER
psychiatric, client and, relationship,
18 *et seq.*
early, 5
role of, 9
training, 8
SOCIOLOGY
understanding of individual in, 12
SPITZ, R., 23
SPLITTING, 45–46, 86, 126, 130
SPOTNITZ, H., 145
STANDARDS
problems in adolescence, 72
STATUTORY REGULATIONS, 127
worker's attitude to, 108
confusion, 149–150
STEPHENS, T., 135

T

TIMMS, N., 10, 39, 147
TOWLE, C., 82, 90, 92
TOYNBEE, H. V., 1
TRASLER, G., 86, 87, 147, 148
TREATMENT
investigation and, 8

V

VAIZEY, J., 43, 155
VISITS
foster parents, routine, 115
VOLUNTARY WORK
inspection, 149

W

WALDRON, F., 143
WEBB, BEATRICE, 1
WEINSTEIN, E. A., 104
WILDE, OSCAR, 59
WILSON, A., 154

WILSON, H., 136
WILLMOTT, P., 13
WILTSE, K. T., 135
WOODHOUSE, D. L., 136
WOOTTON, B., 10, 26, 84
WORDSWORTHS, 79
WORKER
admitting to care, 21 *et seq.*
attitude towards parents, 133, 157–
158
work, 159
authority, appreciation, 144
conflicts, 146
contacts, range, 146
co-operation with residential staff,
155
emotional problems, 157 *et seq.*
expectations, 146
financial dealings, illustration, 128
foster parents, communication with,
99
problems, attitude to,
106
response to, 92
supervision of, 148
guilt, 157
hostility towards, 125
letters, work by means of, 72, 77
relationship, client, 17
colleagues, 153
court, 157
foster parents, 83, 93,
101, 107, 109,
111
child, 101
residential staff, 154,
156
school staff, 141
role, 145
conflicts, 148
definition, 153
disagreement, 150
foster care problems, 103
children's religion, 148
statutory, confusion, 149–150
separating child from parents, 151
"sharing" problems, 157
statutory obligations, foster care, in,
107–108
untrained, 153
And see SOCIAL WORKER

Y

YOUNG, M., 13